# A Midsummer Night's Dream

**and Related Readings**

Glencoe
McGraw-Hill

New York, New York   Columbus, Ohio   Woodland Hills, California   Peoria, Illinois

## Acknowledgments

Grateful acknowledgment is given authors, publishers, photographers, museums, and agents for permission to reprint the following copyrighted material. Every effort has been made to determine copyright owners. In case of any omissions, the Publisher will be pleased to make suitable acknowledgments in future editions.

"Comedy" by Christopher Fry. Copyright © 1951 by Christopher Fry. Reprinted by permission of ACTAC Theatrical & Cinematic, the duly authorized agent of the author.

"Forget the Footnotes! And Other Advice" from THE FRIENDLY SHAKESPEARE by Norrie Epstein. Copyright © 1993 by Norrie Epstein, Jon Winokur, and Reid Boates. Used by permission of Viking Penguin, a division of Penguin Putnam, Inc.

"Based on an original idea by William Shakespeare" by Victoria McKee as published in *The Independent*, April 20, 1996. Reprinted by permission of Victoria McKee.

"Family; Allow Puck to Introduce Kids to Will" by Lynne Heffley, published in the *Los Angeles Times*, April 13, 1998. Copyright © 1998, Los Angeles Times. Reprinted by permission.

"How the Bard Won the West" by Jennifer Lee Carrell. From *Smithsonian* (August 1998). Reprinted by permission of the author.

**Cover Art:** Courtesy Sotheby's Picture Library

*Glencoe/McGraw-Hill*

A Division of The **McGraw·Hill** Companies

Send all inquiries to:
**Glencoe/McGraw-Hill**
8787 Orion Place
Columbus, OH 43240

ISBN 0-02-817958-7
Printed in the United States of America
3 4 5 6 7 8 9 026 04 03 02 01

# Contents

## A Midsummer Night's Dream

## Related Readings 73

*Continued*

Contents *Continued*

# A Midsummer Night's Dream

❧

**William Shakespeare**

# Characters

## The Court

**HIPPOLYTA:** Queen of the Amazons, engaged to Theseus

**THESEUS:** Duke of Athens, engaged to Hippolyta

**EGEUS:** father of Hermia

**PHILOSTRATE:** Master of the Revels to the Athenian Court

## The Lovers

**HERMIA:** in love with Lysander

**HELENA:** in love with Demetrius

**LYSANDER:** in love with Hermia

**DEMETRIUS:** Egeus' choice as a husband for Hermia

## The Mechanicals

**NICK BOTTOM:** a weaver who plays Pyramus

**PETER QUINCE:** a carpenter who speaks the Prologue

**FRANCIS FLUTE:** a bellows-mender who plays Thisbe

**TOM SNOUT:** a tinker who plays Wall

**ROBIN STARVELING:** a tailor who plays Moonshine

**SNUG:** a joiner who plays Lion

## The Fairies

**OBERON:** King of the Fairies

**TITANIA:** Queen of the Fairies

**PUCK (OR ROBIN GOODFELLOW):** Oberon's attendant

**PEASEBLOSSOM**

**COBWEB**
⎫
⎬ Titania's fairy attendants
⎭

**MOTH**

**MUSTARDSEED**

a **FAIRY** in Titania's service

# Act 1

## SCENE 1. Athens. THESEUS' Palace.

[*Enter THESEUS, HIPPOLYTA, PHILOSTRATE, with others.*]

> **THESEUS.**   Now, fair Hippolyta, our nuptial hour
> Draws on apace; four happy days bring in
> Another moon—but O, methinks, how slow
> This old moon wanes! She lingers my desires,
> 5    Like to a step-dame or a dowager°
> Long withering out a young man's revenue.°
>
> **HIPPOLYTA.**   Four days will quickly steep themselves in night;
> Four nights will quickly dream away the time;
> And then the moon, like to a silver bow
> 10    New bent in heaven, shall behold the night
> Of our solemnities.°
>
> **THESEUS.**                Go, Philostrate,
> Stir up the Athenian youth to merriments,
> Awake the pert and nimble spirit of mirth;
> Turn melancholy forth to funerals;
> 15    The pale companion is not for our pomp.

[*Exit PHILOSTRATE.*]

> Hippolyta, I wooed thee with my sword,
> And won thy love doing thee injuries;
> But I will wed thee in another key,
> With pomp, with triumph, and with revelling.

---

5    **dowager**  a widow with money or property
6    **revenue**  wealth
11   **solemnities**  formal ceremonies

[*Enter* EGEUS *and his daughter* HERMIA, LYSANDER, *and* DEMETRIUS.]

20 **EGEUS.**   Happy be Theseus, our renownèd Duke!

**THESEUS.**   Thanks, good Egeus. What's the news with thee?

**EGEUS.**   Full of vexation come I, with complaint
Against my child, my daughter Hermia.
Stand forth, Demetrius!—My noble lord,
25 This man hath my consent to marry her.
Stand forth, Lysander!—And, my gracious Duke,
This man hath bewitched the bosom of my child.
Thou, thou, Lysander, thou hast given her rhymes,
And interchanged love-tokens with my child.
30 Thou hast by moonlight at her window sung
With feigning voice verses of feigning° love,
And stolen the impression of her fantasy,
With bracelets of thy hair, rings, gauds, conceits,°
Knacks, trifles, nosegays, sweetmeats—messengers
35 Of strong prevailment° in unhardened youth;
With cunning hast thou filched° my daughter's heart,
Turned her obedience, which is due to me,
To stubborn harshness. And, my gracious Duke,
Be it so she will not here, before your grace,
40 Consent to marry with Demetrius,
I beg the ancient privilege of Athens;
As she is mine, I may dispose of her;
Which shall be either to this gentleman
Or to her death, according to our law
45 Immediately provided in that case.

**THESEUS.**   What say you, Hermia? Be advised, fair maid.
To you your father should be as a god,
One that composed your beauties; yea, and one
To whom you are but as a form in wax
50 By him imprinted,° and within his power
To leave the figure, or disfigure it.
Demetrius is a worthy gentleman.

---

31   **feigning**  untrue, deceitful
33   **gauds, conceits**  fancy trinkets
35   **prevailment**  pressure
36   **filched**  stolen
50   **imprinted**  molded, stamped

**HERMIA.**   So is Lysander.

**THESEUS.**                    In himself he is;
　　　But in this kind, wanting your father's voice,
55　　The other must be held the worthier.

**HERMIA.**   I would my father looked but with my eyes.

**THESEUS.**   Rather your eyes must with his judgement look.

**HERMIA.**   I do entreat your grace to pardon me.
　　　I know not by what power I am made bold,
60　　Nor how it may concern my modesty
　　　In such a presence here to plead my thoughts;
　　　But I beseech your grace that I may know
　　　The worst that may befall me in this case,
　　　If I refuse to wed Demetrius.

65　**THESEUS.**   Either to die the death, or to abjure
　　　For ever the society of men.
　　　Therefore, fair Hermia, question your desires,
　　　Know of your youth, examine well your blood,
　　　Whether, if you yield not to your father's choice,
70　　You can endure the livery° of a nun,
　　　For aye to be in shady cloister mewed,°
　　　To live a barren sister° all your life,
　　　Chanting faint hymns to the cold fruitless moon.
　　　Thrice blessèd they that master so their blood
75　　To undergo such maiden pilgrimage;
　　　But earthlier happy is the rose distilled
　　　Than that which, withering on the virgin thorn,
　　　Grows, lives, and dies in single blessedness.

**HERMIA.**   So will I grow, so live, so die, my lord,
80　　Ere I will yield my virgin patent up
　　　Unto his lordship, whose unwishèd yoke°
　　　My soul consents not to give sovereignty.

**THESEUS.**   Take time to pause, and by the next new moon,
　　　The sealing-day° betwixt my love and me
85　　For everlasting bond of fellowship,

---

70　**livery** clothes
71　**mewed** confined
72　**barren sister** nun
81　**yoke** constraint
84　**sealing-day** wedding day

Upon that day either prepare to die
For disobedience to your father's will,
Or else to wed Demetrius, as he would,
Or on Diana's altar to protest
90    For aye austerity° and single life.

DEMETRIUS.    Relent, sweet Hermia; and, Lysander, yield
Thy crazèd title to my certain right.

LYSANDER.    You have her father's love, Demetrius;
Let me have Hermia's—do you marry him.

95    EGEUS.    Scornful Lysander, true, he hath my love,
And what is mine my love shall render him;
And she is mine, and all my right of her
I do estate unto° Demetrius.

LYSANDER.    I am, my lord, as well-derived° as he,
100    As well-possessed: my love is more than his,
My fortunes every way as fairly ranked,
If not with vantage,° as Demetrius';
And, which is more than all these boasts can be,
I am beloved of beauteous Hermia.
105    Why should not I then prosecute my right?
Demetrius, I'll avouch it to his head,
Made love to Nedar's daughter, Helena,
And won her soul; and she, sweet lady, dotes,
Devoutly dotes, dotes in idolatry,
110    Upon this spotted and inconstant man.

THESEUS.    I must confess that I have heard so much,
And with Demetrius thought to have spoke thereof;
But, being overfull of self-affairs,
My mind did lose it. But Demetrius, come,
115    And come, Egeus. You shall go with me;
I have some private schooling for you both.
For you, fair Hermia, look you arm yourself
To fit your fancies to your father's will;
Or else the law of Athens yields you up
120    (Which by no means we may extenuate)

---

90    **austerity** self-control, abstinence
98    **estate unto** give to
99    **well-derived** of a good family and background
102    **vantage** advantage

To death, or to a vow of single life.
Come, my Hippolyta; what cheer, my love?
Demetrius and Egeus, go along;
I must employ you in some business
125      Against° our nuptial, and confer with you
Of something nearly that concerns yourselves.

**EGEUS.**   With duty and desire we follow you.

[*Exit all but* LYSANDER *and* HERMIA.]

**LYSANDER.**   How now, my love? Why is your cheek so pale?
How chance the roses there do fade so fast?

130   **HERMIA.**   Belike for want of rain, which I could well
Beteem° them from the tempest of my eyes.

**LYSANDER.**   Ay me! For aught that I could ever read,
Could ever hear by tale or history,
The course of true love never did run smooth;
135      But either it was different in blood—°

**HERMIA.**   O cross! too high to be enthralled° to low.

**LYSANDER.**   Or else misgraffèd° in respect of years—

**HERMIA.**   O spite! too old to be engaged to young.

**LYSANDER.**   Or else it stood upon the choice of friends—

140   **HERMIA.**   O hell, to choose love by another's eyes!

**LYSANDER.**   Or, if there were a sympathy in choice,
War, death, or sickness did lay siege to it,
Making it momentany as a sound,
Swift as a shadow, short as any dream,
145      Brief as the lightning in the collied° night,
That in a spleen° unfolds both heaven and earth,
And, ere a man hath power to say, 'Behold!',
The jaws of darkness do devour it up.
So quick bright things come to confusion.

---

125   **against** in preparation for
131   **beteem** grant
135   **blood** class, family background
136   **enthralled** bound
137   **misgraffèd** mismatched
145   **collied** darkened, like coal
146   **spleen** burst of temper

**HERMIA.**    If then true lovers have been ever crossed
150    It stands as an edict° in destiny.
    Then let us teach our trial patience,
    Because it is a customary cross,
    As due to love as thoughts, and dreams, and sighs,
155    Wishes, and tears—poor fancy's followers.

**LYSANDER.**    A good persuasion. Therefore hear me, Hermia:
    I have a widow aunt, a dowager,
    Of great revenue,° and she hath no child.
    From Athens is her house remote seven leagues;
160    And she respects me as her only son.
    There, gentle Hermia, may I marry thee;
    And to that place the sharp Athenian law
    Cannot pursue us. If thou lov'st me, then
    Steal forth thy father's house tomorrow night,
165    And in the wood, a league° without the town
    (Where I did meet thee once with Helena
    To do observance to a morn of May),
    There will I stay for thee.

**HERMIA.**                              My good Lysander,
    I swear to thee by Cupid's strongest bow,
170    By his best arrow with the golden head,
    By the simplicity of Venus' doves,
    By that which knitteth souls and prospers loves,
    And by that fire which burned the Carthage queen
    When the false Trojan under sail was seen,
175    By all the vows that ever men have broke
    (In number more than ever women spoke),
    In that same place thou hast appointed me,
    Tomorrow truly will I meet with thee.

**LYSANDER.**    Keep promise, love. Look, here comes Helena.

[*Enter* HELENA.]

180    **HERMIA.**    God speed, fair Helena! Whither away?

    **HELENA.**    Call you me fair? That 'fair' again unsay.
    Demetrius loves your fair: O happy fair!

---

151    **edict** command
158    **revenue** wealth
165    **league** about three miles

Your eyes are lodestars,° and your tongue's sweet air
More tuneable than lark to shepherd's ear
185 When wheat is green, when hawthorn buds appear.
Sickness is catching. O, were favour so,
Yours would I catch, fair Hermia, ere I go;
My ear should catch your voice, my eye your eye,
My tongue should catch your tongue's sweet melody.
190 Were the world mine, Demetrius being bated,°
The rest I'd give to be to you translated.
O, teach me how you look and with what art
You sway the motion of Demetrius' heart.

**HERMIA.** I frown upon him; yet he loves me still.

195 **HELENA.** O that your frowns would teach my smiles such skill!

**HERMIA.** I give him curses; yet he gives me love.

**HELENA.** O that my prayers could such affection move!

**HERMIA.** The more I hate, the more he follows me.

**HELENA.** The more I love, the more he hateth me.

200 **HERMIA.** His folly, Helena, is no fault of mine.

**HELENA.** None but your beauty; would that fault were mine!

**HERMIA.** Take comfort: he no more shall see my face;
Lysander and myself will fly this place.
Before the time I did Lysander see,
205 Seemed Athens as a paradise to me.
O then, what graces in my love do dwell,
That he hath turned a heaven unto a hell?

**LYSANDER.** Helen, to you our minds we will unfold:
Tomorrow night, when Phoebe° doth behold
210 Her silver visage in the watery glass,
Decking with liquid pearl the bladed grass
(A time that lovers' flights doth still conceal),
Through Athens' gates have we devised to steal.

**HERMIA.** And in the wood, where often you and I
215 Upon faint primrose beds were wont to lie,
Emptying our bosoms of their counsel sweet,

---

183 **lodestars** guiding stars
190 **bated** excepted
209 **Phoebe** Diana, goddess of the moon, associated with chastity

There my Lysander and myself shall meet,
And thence from Athens turn away our eyes
To seek new friends and stranger companies.
220   Farewell, sweet playfellow; pray thou for us,
And good luck grant thee thy Demetrius.
Keep word, Lysander; we must starve our sight
From lovers' food till morrow deep midnight.

**LYSANDER.**   I will, my Hermia.

[*Exit* HERMIA.]

                                        Helena, adieu!
225   As you on him, Demetrius dote on you.

[*Exit* LYSANDER.]

**HELENA.**   How happy some o'er other some can be!
Through Athens I am thought as fair as she.
But what of that? Demetrius thinks not so;
He will not know what all but he do know.
230   And as he errs, doting on Hermia's eyes,
So I, admiring of his qualities.
Things base and vile, holding no quantity,°
Love can transpose to form and dignity.
Love looks not with the eyes, but with the mind,
235   And therefore is winged Cupid painted blind.
Nor hath love's mind of any judgement taste;
Wings, and no eyes, figure unheedy haste;
And therefore is love said to be a child
Because in choice he is so oft beguiled.°
240   As waggish° boys in game themselves forswear,°
So the boy Love is perjured everywhere;
For, ere Demetrius looked on Hermia's eyne,°
He hailed down oaths that he was only mine,
And when this hail some heat from Hermia felt,
245   So he dissolved, and showers of oaths did melt.
I will go tell him of fair Hermia's flight:
Then to the wood will he, tomorrow night,

---

232   **holding no quantity**  having no value
239   **beguiled**  tricked
240   **waggish**  mischievous
        **forswear**  falsely promise
242   **eyne**  eyes

Pursue her; and for this intelligence,
If I have thanks it is a dear expense;
250 But herein mean I to enrich my pain,
To have his sight thither, and back again.

[*Exit* HELENA.]


## SCENE 2. Athens.

[*Enter* QUINCE *the Carpenter, and* SNUG *the Joiner, and* BOTTOM *the Weaver,
and* FLUTE *the Bellows-mender, and* SNOUT *the Tinker, and* STARVELING *the
Tailor.*]

**QUINCE.** Is all our company here?

**BOTTOM.** You were best to call them generally, man by man,
according to the scrip.

**QUINCE.** Here is the scroll of every man's name which is thought fit
5 through all Athens to play in our interlude before the Duke and
the Duchess on his wedding day at night.

**BOTTOM.** First, good Peter Quince, say what the play treats on;
then read the names of the actors; and so grow to a point.

**QUINCE.** Marry, our play is 'The most lamentable comedy and most
10 cruel death of Pyramus and Thisbe'.

**BOTTOM.** A very good piece of work, I assure you, and a merry.
Now, good Peter Quince, call forth your actors by the scroll.
Masters, spread yourselves.

**QUINCE.** Answer as I call you. Nick Bottom, the weaver?

15 **BOTTOM.** Ready. Name what part I am for, and proceed.

**QUINCE.** You, Nick Bottom, are set down for Pyramus.

**BOTTOM.** What is Pyramus? A lover or a tyrant?

**QUINCE.** A lover that kills himself, most gallant, for love.

**BOTTOM.** That will ask some tears in the true performing of it. If I
do it, let the audience look to their eyes: I will move storms, I will
condole,° in some measure. To the rest—yet my chief humour is
for a tyrant. I could play Ercles° rarely, or a part to tear a cat in,° to
make all split:

> The raging rocks
> And shivering shocks
> Shall break the locks
>   Of prison gates,
> And Phibbus'° car
> Shall shine from far,
> And make and mar
>   The foolish Fates.

This was lofty. Now name the rest of the players.—This is Ercles'
vein, a tyrant's vein; a lover is more condoling.

**QUINCE.** Francis Flute, the bellows-mender?

**FLUTE.** Here, Peter Quince.

**QUINCE.** Flute, you must take Thisbe on you.

**FLUTE.** What is Thisbe? A wandering knight?

**QUINCE.** It is the lady that Pyramus must love.

**FLUTE.** Nay, faith, let not me play a woman: I have a beard coming.

**QUINCE.** That's all one: you shall play it in a mask, and you may
speak as small° as you will.

**BOTTOM.** And I may hide my face, let me play Thisbe too. I'll speak
in a monstrous little voice: 'Thisne, Thisne!' — 'Ah, Pyramus, my
lover dear; thy Thisbe dear, and lady dear.'

**QUINCE.** No, no; you must play Pyramus; and Flute, you Thisbe.

**BOTTOM.** Well, proceed.

**QUINCE.** Robin Starveling, the tailor?

**STARVELING.** Here, Peter Quince.

**QUINCE.** Robin Starveling, you must play Thisbe's mother. Tom
Snout, the tinker?

---

21  **condole**  show grief
22  **Ercles**  Hercules
     **to tear a cat in**  to rant and rave
28  **Phibbus**  Phoebus, god of the sun, who was supposed to drive a chariot ('car') through the sky
40  **small**  high-pitched

**SNOUT.**   Here, Peter Quince.

**QUINCE.**   You, Pyramus' father; myself, Thisbe's father; Snug, the joiner, you the lion's part; and I hope here is a play fitted.

**SNUG.**   Have you the lion's part written? Pray you, if it be, give it
55   me; for I am slow of study.

**QUINCE.**   You may do it extempore;° for it is nothing but roaring.

**BOTTOM.**   Let me play the lion too. I will roar that I will do any man's heart good to hear me. I will roar that I will make the Duke say 'Let him roar again, let him roar again!'

60   **QUINCE.**   And you should do it too terribly, you would fright the Duchess and the ladies that they would shriek; and that were enough to hang us all.

**ALL.**   They would hang us, every mother's son.

**BOTTOM.**   I grant you, friends, if you should fright the ladies out of
65   their wits they would have no more discretion but to hang us; but I will aggravate my voice so that I will roar you as gently as any sucking dove. I will roar you and 'twere any nightingale.

**QUINCE.**   You can play no part but Pyramus; for Pyramus is a sweet-faced man, a proper man as one shall see in a summer's day, a most
70   lovely, gentlemanlike man: therefore you must needs play Pyramus.

**BOTTOM.**   Well, I will undertake it. What beard were I best to play it in?

**QUINCE.**   Why, what you will.

**BOTTOM.**   I will discharge it in either your straw-colour beard, your
75   orange-tawny beard, your purple-in-grain beard, or your French-crown-colour beard, your perfect yellow.

**QUINCE.**   Some of your French crowns° have no hair at all, and then you will play bare-faced. But, masters, here are your parts, and I am to entreat you, request you, and desire you to con° them by
80   tomorrow night, and meet me in the palace wood, a mile without the town, by moonlight; there will we rehearse, for if we meet in the city we shall be dogged with company,° and our devices

---

56   **extempore** ad lib
77   **French crown** bald
79   **con** learn
82   **be dogged with company** have people watching

known. In the meantime I will draw a bill of properties, such as our play wants. I pray you, fail me not.

85 **BOTTOM.** We will meet, and there we may rehearse most obscenely and courageously. Take pains, be perfect: adieu!

**QUINCE.** At the Duke's oak we meet.

**BOTTOM.** Enough; hold, or cut bowstrings.

[*They exit.*]

# Act 2

**SCENE 1. The wood.**

[*Enter a* FAIRY *at one door, and* PUCK, *or* ROBIN GOODFELLOW *at another.*]

    PUCK.   How now, spirit; whither wander you?

    FAIRY.   Over hill, over dale,
        Thorough bush, thorough briar,
     Over park, over pale,°
5         Thorough flood, thorough fire;
     I do wander everywhere
     Swifter than the moon's sphere;
     And I serve the Fairy Queen,
     To dew her orbs upon the green.
10    The cowslips tall her pensioners be;
     In their gold coats spots you see—
     Those be rubies, fairy favours,
     In those freckles live their savours.
       I must go seek some dewdrops here,
15      And hang a pearl in every cowslip's ear.
     Farewell, thou lob° of spirits; I'll be gone.
     Our Queen and all her elves come here anon.

    PUCK.   The King doth keep his revels here tonight.
     Take heed the Queen come not within his sight,
20    For Oberon is passing fell and wrath,°
     Because that she as her attendant hath
     A lovely boy stol'n from an Indian king;
     She never had so sweet a changeling,°

---

    4   **pale** fence
  16   **lob** lout
  20   **passing . . . wrath** very fierce and angry
  23   **changeling** a child stolen by fairies

And jealous Oberon would have the child
25    Knight of his train, to trace the forests wild.
      But she perforce withholds the lovèd boy,
      Crowns him with flowers, and makes him all her joy.
      And now they never meet in grove or green,
      By fountain clear or spangled starlight sheen,
30    But they do square,° that all their elves for fear
      Creep into acorn cups and hide them there.

      FAIRY.   Either I mistake your shape and making quite,
      Or else you are that shrewd° and knavish sprite
      Called Robin Goodfellow. Are not you he
35    That frights the maidens of the villagery,
      Skim milk,° and sometimes labour in the quern,°
      And bootless° make the breathless housewife churn,
      And sometimes make the drink to bear no barm,°
      Mislead night-wanderers, laughing at their harm?
40    Those that 'Hobgoblin' call you, and 'Sweet Puck',
      You do their work, and they shall have good luck.
      Are not you he?

      PUCK.                  Thou speakest aright;
      I am that merry wanderer of the night.
      I jest to Oberon, and make him smile
45    When I a fat and bean-fed horse beguile,
      Neighing in likeness of a filly foal;
      And sometime lurk I in a gossip's bowl
      In very likeness of a roasted crab,°
      And when she drinks, against her lips I bob,
50    And on her withered dewlap pour the ale.
      The wisest aunt, telling the saddest tale,
      Sometime for threefoot stool mistaketh me;
      Then slip I from her bum, down topples she,
      And 'Tailor' cries, and falls into a cough;

---

30    **square**  quarrel
33    **shrewd**  evil or mischievous
36    **skim milk**  skim off the cream
      **quern**  hand mill for grinding corn
37    **bootless**  pointless
38    **barm**  the head on beer
48    **crab**  crab apple

55    And then the whole choir hold their hips and loffe,°
      And waxen in their mirth, and neeze, and swear
      A merrier hour was never wasted there.
      But room, Fairy: here comes Oberon.

      **FAIRY.**    And here my mistress. Would that he were gone!

[*Enter* OBERON, *the King of Fairies, at one door, with his train; and* TITANIA, *the Queen, at another with hers.*]

60    **OBERON.**    Ill met by moonlight, proud Titania!

      **TITANIA.**    What, jealous Oberon? Fairies, skip hence.
      I have forsworn his bed and company.

      **OBERON.**    Tarry,° rash wanton! Am not I thy lord?°

      **TITANIA.**    Then I must be thy lady.° But I know
65    When thou hast stol'n away from Fairyland,
      And in the shape of Corin° sat all day
      Playing on pipes of corn, and versing love
      To amorous Phillida.° Why are thou here
      Come from the farthest step of India?—
70    But that, forsooth, the bouncing Amazon,
      Your buskined° mistress and your warrior love,
      To Theseus must be wedded; and you come
      To give their bed joy and prosperity.

      **OBERON.**    How canst thou thus, for shame, Titania,
75    Glance at my credit with Hippolyta,
      Knowing I know thy love to Theseus?
      Didst not thou lead him through the glimmering night
      From Perigenia,° whom he ravishèd,
      And make him with fair Aegles° break his faith,
80    With Ariadne,° and Antiopa?°

      **TITANIA.**    These are the forgeries of jealousy:
      And never since the middle summer's spring
      Met we on hill, in dale, forest, or mead,
      By pavèd fountain or by rushy brook,

---

| 55 | **loffe** laugh |
| 63 | **tarry** wait |
| 63–4 | **lord, lady** they are husband and wife |
| 66, 68 | **Corin, Phillida** two mythical lovers |
| 71 | **buskined** wearing hunting boots |
| 78, 79, 80 | **Perigenia, Aegles, Ariadne, Antiopa** women Theseus had known |

85      Or in the beachèd margent° of the sea
        To dance our ringlets° to the whistling wind,
        But with thy brawls thou hast disturbed our sport.
        Therefore the winds, piping to us in vain,
        As in revenge have sucked up from the sea
90      Contagious fogs; which, falling in the land,
        Hath every pelting river made so proud
        That they have overborne their continents.
        The ox hath therefore stretched his yoke in vain,
        The ploughman lost his sweat, and the green corn
95      Hath rotted ere his youth attained a beard.
        The fold stands empty in the drownèd field,
        And crows are fatted with the murrion flock;°
        The nine-men's-morris° is filled up with mud,
        And the quaint mazes in the wanton green
100     For lack of tread are undistinguishable.
        The human mortals want their winter cheer;
        No night is now with hymn or carol blessed.
        Therefore the moon, the governess of floods,
        Pale in her anger, washes all the air,
105     That rheumatic diseases do abound;
        And thorough this distemperature° we see
        The seasons alter; hoary-headed frosts
        Fall in the fresh lap of the crimson rose,
        And on old Hiems'° thin and icy crown
110     An odorous chaplet of sweet summer buds
        Is, as in mockery, set. The spring, the summer,
        The childing° autumn, angry winter change
        Their wonted liveries, and the mazèd° world
        By their increase now knows not which is which.
115     And this same progeny of evils comes
        From our debate, from our dissension.
        We are their parents and original.

---

| 85 | **beachèd margent** shore |
| 86 | **ringlets** dancing in a circle |
| 97 | **murrion flock** diseased sheep |
| 98 | **nine-men's-morris** an outdoor gam |
| 106 | **distemperature** disorder |
| 109 | **old Hiems** winter |
| 112 | **childing** pregnant, fruitful |
| 113 | **mazèd** amazed, confused |

**OBERON.** Do you amend it, then: it lies in you.
Why should Titania cross her Oberon?
120 I do but beg a little changeling boy
To be my henchman.°

**TITANIA.** Set your heart at rest.
The fairy land buys not the child of me.
His mother was a votress° of my order,
And in the spicèd Indian air by night
125 Full often hath she gossiped by my side,
And sat with me on Neptune's yellow sands
Marking th'embarkèd traders on the flood,
When we have laughed to see the sails conceive
And grow big-bellied with the wanton° wind;
130 Which she, with pretty and with swimming gait
Following (her womb then rich with my young squire),
Would imitate, and sail upon the land
To fetch me trifles, and return again
As from a voyage, rich with merchandise.
135 But she, being mortal, of that boy did die,
And for her sake do I rear up her boy;
And for her sake I will not part with him.

**OBERON.** How long within this wood intend you stay?

**TITANIA.** Perchance till after Theseus' wedding day.
140 If you will patiently dance in our round,
And see our moonlight revels, go with us:
If not, shun me, and I will spare your haunts.

**OBERON.** Give me that boy, and I will go with thee.

**TITANIA.** Not for thy fairy kingdom! Fairies, away.
145 We shall chide° downright if I longer stay.

[*Exit* TITANIA *and her train.*]

---

121 **henchman** page
123 **votress** member of religious order, worshipper
129 **wanton** mischievous, immoral
145 **chide** argue, criticize

OBERON.    Well, go thy way. Thou shalt not from this grove
    Till I torment thee for this injury.
    My gentle Puck, come hither. Thou rememberest
    Since once I sat upon a promontory,
150    And heard a mermaid on a dolphin's back
    Uttering such dulcet° and harmonious breath
    That the rude sea grew civil at her song,
    And certain stars shot madly from their spheres°
    To hear the sea-maid's music?

PUCK.                          I remember.

155  OBERON.    That very time I saw (but thou couldst not)
    Flying between the cold moon and the earth
    Cupid all armed: a certain aim he took
    At a fair vestal thronèd by the west,
    And loosed his loveshaft smartly from his bow
160    As it should pierce a hundred thousand hearts;
    But I might see young Cupid's fiery shaft°
    Quenched in the chaste beams of the watery moon;
    And the imperial votress passèd on
    In maiden meditation, fancy-free.
165    Yet marked I where the bolt° of Cupid fell:
    It fell upon  a little western flower,
    Before, milk-white; now purple with love's wound:
    And maidens call it 'love-in-idleness'.
    Fetch me that flower, the herb I showed thee once;
170    The juice of it on sleeping eyelids laid
    Will make or man or woman madly dote
    Upon the next live creature that it sees.
    Fetch me this herb, and be thou here again
    Ere the leviathan° can swim a league.

175  PUCK.    I'll put a girdle round about the earth
    In forty minutes!

[*Exit* PUCK.]

---

151    **dulcet**  soothing, quiet
153    **spheres**  orbits
161    **Cupid's fiery shaft**  Cupid's arrow, which was supposed to make the person that it hit fall in love
165    **bolt**  arrow
174    **leviathan**  whale

**OBERON.**                              Having once this juice
        I'll watch Titania when she is asleep,
        And drop the liquor of it in her eyes:
        The next thing then she, waking, looks upon—
180     Be it on lion, bear, or wolf, or bull,
        On meddling monkey, or on busy ape—
        She shall pursue it with the soul of love.
        And ere I take this charm from off her sight
        (As I can take it with another herb)
185     I'll make her render up her page to me.
        But who comes here? I am invisible,
        And I will overhear their conference.

[*Enter* DEMETRIUS, HELENA *following him.*]

**DEMETRIUS.**    I love thee not, therefore pursue me not.
        Where is Lysander, and fair Hermia?
190     The one I'll slay, the other slayeth me.
        Thou told'st me they were stol'n unto this wood,
        And here am I, and wood within this wood°
        Because I cannot meet my Hermia.
        Hence, get thee gone, and follow me no more.

195     **HELENA.**    You draw me, you hard-heart adamant!°
        But yet you draw not iron, for my heart
        Is true as steel. Leave you your power to draw,
        And I shall have no power to follow you.

        **DEMETRIUS.**    Do I entice you? Do I speak you fair?
200     Or rather do I not in plainest truth
        Tell you I do not, nor I cannot love you?

        **HELENA.**    And even for that do I love you the more.
        I am your spaniel; and, Demetrius,
        The more you beat me I will fawn on you.
205     Use me but as your spaniel: spurn me, strike me,
        Neglect me, lose me; only give me leave,
        Unworthy as I am, to follow you.
        What worser place can I beg in your love
        (And yet a place of high respect with me)
210     Than to be usèd as you use your dog?

---

192    **wood** mad, insane while he is in a real wood. Elizabethans were fond of wordplay
       and puns
195    **adamant** hard stone, diamond

DEMETRIUS.    Tempt not too much the hatred of my spirit;
　　For I am sick when I do look on thee.

HELENA.    And I am sick when I look not on you.

DEMETRIUS.    You do impeach° your modesty too much,
215　To leave the city and commit yourself
　　Into the hands of one that loves you not;
　　To trust the opportunity of night,
　　And the ill counsel of a desert° place,
　　With the rich worth of your virginity.

220　HELENA.    Your virtue is my privilege: for that
　　It is not night when I do see your face,
　　Therefore I think I am not in the night;
　　Nor doth this wood lack worlds of company,
　　For you, in my respect, are all the world.
225　Then how can it be said I am alone
　　When all the world is here to look on me?

DEMETRIUS.    I'll run from thee and hide me in the brakes,°
　　And leave thee to the mercy of wild beasts.

HELENA.    The wildest hath not such a heart as you.
230　Run when you will: the story shall be changed;
　　Apollo flies, and Daphne holds the chase,
　　The dove pursues the griffin,° the mild hind
　　Makes speed to catch the tiger—bootless° speed,
　　When cowardice pursues, and valour flies!

235　DEMETRIUS.    I will not stay thy questions. Let me go;
　　Or if thou follow me, do not believe
　　But I shall do thee mischief in the wood.

HELENA.    Ay, in the temple, in the town, the field,
　　You do me mischief. Fie, Demetrius,
240　Your wrongs do set a scandal on my sex!
　　We cannot fight for love, as men may do;
　　We shall be wooed, and were not made to woo.

[*Exit* DEMETRIUS.]

---

　214　**impeach**  call into question
　218　**desert**  lonely, deserted
　227　**brakes**  undergrowth, thicket
　232　**griffin**  beast, half eagle, half lion
　233　**bootless**  useless

I'll follow thee, and make a heaven of hell,
To die upon the hand I love so well.

[*Exit* HELENA.]

245   **OBERON.**   Fare thee well, nymph. Ere° he do leave this grove
Thou shalt fly him, and he shall seek thy love.

[*Enter* PUCK.]

Hast thou the flower there? Welcome, wanderer.

**PUCK.**   Ay, there it is.

**OBERON.**                 I pray thee give it me.
I know a bank where the wild thyme blows,
250   Where oxlips and the nodding violet grows,
Quite overcanopied with luscious woodbine,
With sweet musk-roses, and with eglantine:
There sleeps Titania sometime of the night,
Lulled in these flowers with dances and delight;
255   And there the snake throws her enamelled skin,
Weed° wide enough to wrap a fairy in;
And with the juice of this I'll streak her eyes,
And make her full of hateful fantasies.
Take thou some of it, and seek through this grove:
260   A sweet Athenian lady is in love
With a disdainful youth; anoint his eyes,
But do it when the next thing he espies
May be the lady. Thou shalt know the man
By the Athenian garments he hath on.
265   Effect it with some care, that he may prove
More fond on her than she upon her love.
And look thou meet me ere the first cock crow.

**PUCK.**   Fear not, my lord; your servant shall do so.

[*They exit.*]

---

245   **ere** before
256   **weed** cloth

## SCENE 2. The wood.

[*Enter* TITANIA, *Queen of Fairies, with her train.*]

      **TITANIA.**   Come, now a roundel° and a fairy song,
          Then for the third part of a minute, hence—
          Some to kill cankers in the musk-rose buds,
          Some war with reremice° for their leathern wings
5         To make my small elves coats, and some keep back
          The clamorous owl that nightly hoots and wonders
          At our quaint spirits. Sing me now asleep;
          Then to your offices, and let me rest.

[*FAIRIES sing.*]

      **FIRST FAIRY.**   You spotted snakes with double tongue,
10              Thorny hedgehogs, be not seen.
            Newts and blindworms, do no wrong,
              Come not near our Fairy Queen.

      **CHORUS.**       Philomel° with melody
            Sing in our sweet lullaby,
15         Lulla, lulla, lullaby; lulla, lulla, lullaby.
            Never harm
            Nor spell nor charm
         Come our lovely lady nigh.
         So good night, with lullaby.

20    **FIRST FAIRY.**   Weaving spiders, come not here;
              Hence, you longlegged spinners, hence!
            Beetles black approach not near;
              Worm, nor snail, do no offence.

      **CHORUS.**       Philomel with melody
25           Sing in our sweet lullaby,
         Lulla, lulla, lullaby; lulla, lulla, lullaby.
            Never harm
            Nor spell nor charm
         Come our lovely lady nigh.
30         So good night, with lullaby.

[*TITANIA sleeps.*]

---

   1   **roundel**  a dance in a circle
   4   **reremice**  bats
  13   **philomel**  nightingale

**SECOND FAIRY.**    Hence, away! Now all is well;
　　　One aloof stand sentinel!

[*Exit* FAIRIES.]

[*Enter* OBERON; *he squeezes the juice on* TITANIA'S *eyes.*]

　　　**OBERON.**    What thou seest when thou dost wake,
　　　　Do it for thy true love take;
35　　　Love and languish for his sake.
　　　　Be it ounce° or cat or bear,
　　　　Pard,° or boar with bristled hair
　　　　In thy eye that shall appear
　　　　When thou wak'st, it is thy dear.
40　　　Wake when some vile thing is near!

[*Exit* OBERON.]

[*Enter* LYSANDER *and* HERMIA.]

　　　**LYSANDER.**    Fair love, you faint with wandering in the wood,
　　　　And, to speak truth, I have forgot our way.
　　　　We'll rest us, Hermia, if you think it good,
　　　　And tarry for the comfort of the day.

45　　**HERMIA.**    Be it so, Lysander; find you out a bed,
　　　　For I upon this bank will rest my head.

　　　**LYSANDER.**    One turf shall serve as pillow for us both;
　　　　One heart, one bed, two bosoms, and one troth.°

　　　**HERMIA.**    Nay, good Lysander, for my sake, my dear,
50　　　Lie further off yet; do not lie so near.

　　　**LYSANDER.**    O take the sense, sweet, of my innocence!
　　　　Love takes the meaning in love's conference;
　　　　I mean that my heart unto yours is knit,
　　　　So that but one heart we can make of it:
55　　　Two bosoms interchainèd with an oath,
　　　　So then two bosoms and a single troth.
　　　　Then by your side no bed-room me deny,
　　　　For lying so, Hermia, I do not lie.

---

36　**ounce** lynx
37　**pard** leopard
48　**troth** truth

**HERMIA.**     Lysander riddles very prettily.
60     Now much beshrew° my manners and my pride
         If Hermia meant to say Lysander lied.
         But, gentle friend, for love and courtesy
         Lie further off, in human modesty;
         Such separation as may well be said
65     Becomes a virtuous bachelor and a maid,
         So far be distant, and good night, sweet friend;
         Thy love ne'er alter till thy sweet life end!

**LYSANDER.**     Amen, amen, to that fair prayer say I,
         And then end life when I end loyalty!
70     Here is my bed; sleep give thee all his rest.

**HERMIA.**     With half that wish the wisher's eyes be pressed.

[*They sleep.*]

[*Enter* PUCK.]

**PUCK.**          Through the forest have I gone,
                       But Athenian found I none
                       On whose eyes I might approve°
75                   This flower's force in stirring love.
                       Night and silence—Who is here?
                       Weeds° of Athens he doth wear:
                       This is he my master said
                       Despisèd the Athenian maid;
80                   And here the maiden, sleeping sound
                       On the dank and dirty ground.
                       Pretty soul, she durst not lie
                       Near this lack-love, this kill-courtesy.
                       Churl,° upon thy eyes I throw
85                   All the power this charm doth owe.
                       [*He squeezes the juice on* LYSANDER'S *eyes.*]
                       When thou wak'st let love forbid
                       Sleep his seat on thy eyelid.
                       So, awake when I am gone;
                       For I must now to Oberon.

[*Exit* PUCK.]

---

60     **much beshrew**  a curse upon
74     **approve**  put to the proof
77     **weeds**  clothes
84     **churl**  heartless rogue

[*Enter* DEMETRIUS *and* HELENA, *running.*]

90     **HELENA.**   Stay, though thou kill me, sweet Demetrius!

    **DEMETRIUS.**   I charge thee, hence, and do not haunt me thus.

    **HELENA.**   O wilt thou darkling° leave me? Do not so!

    **DEMETRIUS.**   Stay, on thy peril; I alone will go.

[*Exit* DEMETRIUS.]

    **HELENA.**   O, I am out of breath in this fond° chase!
95     The more my prayer, the lesser is my grace.
    Happy is Hermia, wheresoe'er she lies,
    For she hath blessèd and attractive eyes.
    How came her eyes so bright? Not with salt tears—
    If so, my eyes are oftener washed than hers.
100     No, no, I am as ugly as a bear,
    For beasts that meet me run away for fear.
    Therefore no marvel though Demetrius
    Do as a monster fly my presence thus.
    What wicked and dissembling glass of mine
105     Made me compare with Hermia's sphery° eyne?
    But who is here?—Lysander, on the ground?
    Dead, or asleep? I see no blood, no wound.
    Lysander, if you live, good sir, awake!

    **LYSANDER.**   [*Waking.*]
    And run through fire I will for thy sweet sake!
110     Transparent° Helena, nature shows art
    That through thy bosom makes me see thy heart.
    Where is Demetrius? O, how fit a word
    Is that vile name to perish on my sword!

    **HELENA.**   Do not say so, Lysander, say not so.
115     What though he love your Hermia? Lord, what though?
    Yet Hermia still loves you; then be content.

    **LYSANDER.**   Content with Hermia? No; I do repent
    The tedious minutes I with her have spent.
    Not Hermia, but Helena I love.
120     Who will not change a raven for a dove?

---

    92   **darkling**  sad, downcast
    94   **fond**  foolish
   105   **sphery**  star-like
   110   **transparent**  honest, open

The will of man is by his reason swayed,
And reason says you are the worthier maid.
Things growing are not ripe until their season;
So I, being young, till now ripe not to reason.
125 And touching now the point of human skill,
Reason becomes the marshal to my will.
And leads me to your eyes, where I o'erlook
Love's stories written in love's richest book.

HELENA.    Wherefore was I to this keen mockery born?
130 When at your hands did I deserve this scorn?
Is't not enough, is't not enough, young man,
That I did never, no, nor never can
Deserve a sweet look from Demetrius' eye
But you must flout° my insufficiency?
135 Good troth, you do me wrong, good sooth, you do,
In such disdainful manner me to woo!
But fare you well: perforce I must confess
I thought you lord of more true gentleness.
O, that a lady of one man refused
140 Should of another therefore be abused!

[Exit HELENA.]

LYSANDER.    She sees not Hermia. Hermia, sleep thou there,
And never mayst thou come Lysander near.
For, as a surfeit° of the sweetest things
The deepest loathing to the stomach brings,
145 Or as the heresies that men do leave
Are hated most of those they did deceive,
So thou, my surfeit and my heresy,°
Of all be hated, but the most of me!
And, all my powers, address your love and might
150 To honour Helen, and to be her knight.

[Exit LYSANDER.]

HERMIA.    [Waking.]
Help me, Lysander, help me! Do thy best
To pluck this crawling serpent from my breast!
Ay me, for pity! What a dream was here!

---

134    **flout**  mock
143    **surfeit**  surplus, too much
147    **heresy**  false religious belief

Lysander, look how I do quake with fear—
155 Methought a serpent ate my heart away,
And you sat smiling at his cruel prey.
Lysander! What, removed? Lysander, lord!
What, out of hearing? Gone? No sound, no word?
Alack where are you? Speak and if you hear.
160 Speak, of all loves! I swoon almost with fear.
No? Then I well perceive you are not nigh.
Either death or you I'll find immediately.

[*Exit* HERMIA.]

# Act 3

## SCENE 1. The wood.

[*Enter the Clowns,* BOTTOM, QUINCE, SNOUT, STARVELING, SNUG *and* FLUTE. TITANIA *remains on stage, asleep.*]

**BOTTOM.** Are we all met?

**QUINCE.** Pat, pat;° and here's a marvellous convenient place for our rehearsal. This green plot shall be our stage, this hawthorn brake° our tiring-house, and we will do it in action as we will do it before the Duke.

5

**BOTTOM.** Peter Quince!

**QUINCE.** What sayest thou, bully° Bottom?

**BOTTOM.** There are things in this comedy of Pyramus and Thisbe that will never please. First, Pyramus must draw a sword to kill himself, which the ladies cannot abide. How answer you that?

10

**SNOUT.** By'r lakin,° a parlous fear!

**STARVELING.** I believe we must leave the killing out, when all is done.

**BOTTOM.** Not a whit; I have a device to make all well. Write me a prologue, and let the prologue seem to say we will do no harm with our swords, and that Pyramus is not killed indeed; and for the more better assurance, tell them that I, Pyramus, am not Pyramus, but Bottom the weaver: this will put them out of fear.

15

**QUINCE.** Well, we will have such a prologue; and it shall be written in eight and six.

20 **BOTTOM.** No, make it two more: let it be written in eight and eight.

---

2 **Pat** on the dot, on time
3 **brake** thicket
7 **bully** adjective that implies respect and admiration
11 **by'r lakin** by our lady (an exclamation)

**SNOUT.**   Will not the ladies be afeard of the lion?

**STARVELING.**   I fear it, I promise you.

**BOTTOM.**   Masters, you ought to consider with yourself, to bring in (God shield us!) a lion among ladies is a most dreadful thing; for there is not a more fearful wildfowl than your lion living; and we ought to look to't.

**SNOUT.**   Therefore another prologue must tell he is not a lion.

**BOTTOM.**   Nay, you must name his name, and half his face must be seen through the lion's neck, and he himself must speak through, saying thus, or to the same defect: 'Ladies', or 'Fair ladies, I would wish you', or 'I would request you', or 'I would entreat you, not to fear, not to tremble: my life for yours. If you think I come hither as a lion, it were pity of my life. No, I am no such thing; I am a man, as other men are'—and there indeed let him name his name, and tell them plainly he is Snug the joiner.

**QUINCE.**   Well, it shall be so. But there is two hard things: that is, to bring the moonlight into a chamber; for, you know, Pyramus and Thisbe meet by moonlight.

**SNUG.**   Doth the moon shine that night we play our play?

**BOTTOM.**   A calendar, a calendar! Look in the almanac—find out moonshine, find out moonshine!

**QUINCE.**   Yes, it doth shine that night.

**BOTTOM.**   Why, then may you leave a casement of the great chamber window, where we play, open, and the moon may shine in at the casement.°

**QUINCE.**   Ay; or else one must come in with a bush of thorns and a lantern, and say he comes to disfigure, or to present the person of Moonshine. Then there is another thing; we must have a wall in the great chamber; for Pyramus and Thisbe, says the story, did talk through the chink of a wall.

**SNOUT.**   You can never bring in a wall. What say you, Bottom?

**BOTTOM.**   Some man or other must present Wall; and let him have some plaster, or some loam, or some rough-cast about him to signify Wall; or let him hold his fingers thus, and through that cranny shall Pyramus and Thisbe whisper.

---

45   **casement**  hinged window

QUINCE.    If that may be, then all is well. Come, sit down every mother's son, and rehearse your parts. Pyramus, you begin. When you have spoken your speech, enter into that brake, and so everyone according to his cue.

[*Enter* PUCK.]

60    PUCK.    What hempen homespuns° have we swaggering here
So near the cradle of the Fairy Queen?
What, a play toward? I'll be an auditor,
An actor too perhaps, if I see cause.

QUINCE.    Speak, Pyramus! Thisbe, stand forth!

BOTTOM.    [*as Pyramus.*]
65    Thisbe, the flowers of odious savours sweet—

QUINCE.    Odours—'odorous'!

BOTTOM.    [*as Pyramus.*]        . . . odours savours sweet.
So hath thy breath, my dearest Thisbe dear.
But hark, a voice! Stay thou but here awhile,
70        And by and by I will to thee appear.

[*Exit* BOTTOM.]

PUCK.    A stranger Pyramus than e'er played here.

[*Exit* PUCK.]

FLUTE.    Must I speak now?

QUINCE.    Ay, marry must you; for you must understand he goes but to see a noise that he heard, and is to come again.

FLUTE.    [*as Thisbe.*]
75    Most radiant Pyramus, most lilywhite of hue,
Of colour like the red rose on triumphant briar,
Most brisky juvenal, and eke° most lovely Jew,
As true as truest horse that yet would never tire,
I'll meet thee, Pyramus, at Ninny's tomb—

80    QUINCE.    'Ninus' tomb', man!—Why, you must not speak that yet; that you answer to Pyramus. You speak all your part at once, cues and all. Pyramus, enter—your cue is past. It is 'never tire'.

---

60    **hempen homespuns**  they are dressed in rough, homemade clothes
77    **eke**  also

**FLUTE.**   O—
[*as Thisbe.*]
As true as truest horse, that yet would never tire.

[*Enter* PUCK, *and* BOTTOM *with the ass head on.*]

**BOTTOM.**   [*as Pyramus.*]
85   If I were fair, fair Thisbe, I were only thine.

**QUINCE.**   O monstrous! O strange! We are haunted! Pray, masters,
fly, masters! Help!

[*Exit* QUINCE, SNUG, FLUTE, SNOUT, *and* STARVELING.]

**PUCK.**   I'll follow you: I'll lead you about a round,
   Through bog, through bush, through brake, through briar;
90   Sometime a horse I'll be, sometime a hound,
      A hog, a headless bear, sometime a fire,
   And neigh, and bark, and grunt, and roar, and burn,
   Like horse, hound, hog, bear, fire at every turn.

[*Exit* PUCK.]

**BOTTOM.**   Why do they run away? This is a knavery of them to make
95   me afeard.

[*Enter* SNOUT.]

**SNOUT.**   O Bottom, thou art changed. What do I see on thee?

**BOTTOM.**   What do you see? You see an ass head of your own, do you?

[*Exit* SNOUT; *enter* QUINCE.]

**QUINCE.**   Bless thee, Bottom, bless thee! Thou art translated!

[*Exit* QUINCE.]

**BOTTOM.**   I see their knavery. This is to make an ass of me, to fright
100   me, if they could; but I will not stir from this place, do what they
   can. I will walk up and down here, and will sing, that they shall
   hear I am not afraid.
   [*Sings.*] The ousel° cock° so black of hue,
      With orange-tawny bill,
105   The throstle° with his note so true,
      The wren with little quill—

**TITANIA.**   [*Waking.*] What angel wakes me from my flowery bed?

---

103   **ousel** blackbird
      **cock** male bird
105   **throstle** song thrush

**BOTTOM.**  [*Sings.*]  The finch, the sparrow, and the lark,
   The plainsong cuckoo grey,
110    Whose note full many a man doth mark
    And dares not answer nay—
  for indeed, who would set his wit to° so foolish a bird? Who would
  give a bird the lie,° though he cry 'cuckoo' never so?

**TITANIA.**  I pray thee, gentle mortal, sing again;
115  Mine ear is much enamoured of thy note.
  So is mine eye enthrallèd to thy shape,
  And thy fair virtue's force perforce doth move me
  On the first view to say, to swear, I love thee.

**BOTTOM.**  Methinks, mistress, you should have little reason for that.
120  And yet, to say the truth, reason and love keep little company
  together nowadays; the more the pity that some honest neighbours
  will not make them friends. Nay, I can gleek° upon occasion.

**TITANIA.**  Thou art as wise as thou art beautiful.

**BOTTOM.**  Not so neither; but if I had wit enough to get out of this
125  wood, I have enough to serve mine own turn.

**TITANIA.**  Out of this wood do not desire to go:
  Thou shalt remain here, whether thou wilt or no.
  I am a spirit of no common rate;
  The summer still doth tend upon my state,
130  And I do love thee. Therefore go with me.
  I'll give thee fairies to attend on thee,
  And they shall fetch thee jewels from the deep,
  And sing, while thou on pressèd flowers dost sleep;
  And I will purge thy mortal grossness° so
135  That thou shalt like an airy spirit go.
  Peaseblossom, Cobweb, Moth, and Mustardseed!

[*Enter four* FAIRIES.]

**PEASEBLOSSOM.**  Ready.

**COBWEB.**  And I.

**MOTH.**  And I.

---

 112 **set his wit to**  set his wits against, argue with
 113 **give . . . the lie**  contradict, call a liar
 122 **gleek**  joke
 134 **purge . . . grossness**  remove human coarseness

140 **MUSTARDSEED.** And I.

**ALL.** Where shall we go?

**TITANIA.** Be kind and courteous to this gentleman:
  Hop in his walks and gambol in his eyes;
  Feed him with apricocks and dewberries,
145 With purple grapes, green figs, and mulberries;
  The honey-bags steal from the humble-bees,
  And for night-tapers crop their waxen thighs,
  And light them at the fiery glow-worms' eyes
  To have my love to bed, and to arise;
150 And pluck the wings from painted butterflies
  To fan the moonbeams from his sleeping eyes.
  Nod to him, elves, and do him courtesies.

**PEASEBLOSSOM.** Hail, mortal!

**COBWEB.** Hail!

155 **MOTH.** Hail!

**MUSTARDSEED.** Hail!

**BOTTOM.** I cry your worship's mercy, heartily. I beseech your
  worship's name.

**COBWEB.** Cobweb.

160 **BOTTOM.** I shall desire you of more acquaintance, good Master
  Cobweb; if I cut my finger I shall make bold with you. Your name,
  honest gentleman?

**PEASEBLOSSOM.** Peaseblossom.

**BOTTOM.** I pray you commend me to Mistress Squash, your mother,
165 and to Master Peascod, your father. Good Master Peaseblossom,
  I shall desire you of more acquaintance, too.—Your name, I
  beseech you, sir?

**MUSTARDSEED.** Mustardseed.

**BOTTOM.** Good Master Mustardseed, I know your patience well.
170 That same cowardly, giant-like ox-beef hath devoured many a
  gentleman of your house. I promise you, your kindred hath made
  my eyes water ere now. I desire you of more acquaintance, good
  Master Mustardseed.

**TITANIA.** Come, wait upon him. Lead him to my bower.
175   The moon methinks looks with a watery eye,
  And when she weeps, weeps every little flower,

Lamenting some enforcèd chastity.
Tie up my lover's tongue; bring him silently.

[*They exit.*]


## SCENE 2. The wood.

[*Enter* OBERON, *King of Fairies.*]

    **OBERON.**    I wonder if Titania be awaked;
    Then what it was that next came in her eye,
    Which she must dote on, in extremity.

[*Enter* PUCK.]

    Here comes my messenger. How now, mad spirit?
5    What night-rule now about this haunted grove?

    **PUCK.**    My mistress with a monster is in love.
    Near to her close and consecrated bower,
    While she was in her dull and sleeping hour,
    A crew of patches,° rude mechanicals,
10    That work for bread upon Athenian stalls,
    Were met together to rehearse a play
    Intended for great Theseus' nuptial day.
    The shallowest thick-skin of that barren sort,
    Who Pyramus presented, in their sport
15    Forsook his scene and entered in a brake,
    When I did him at this advantage take:
    An ass's nole° I fixèd on his head.
    Anon his Thisbe must be answerèd,
    And forth my mimic comes. When they him spy—
20    As wild geese that the creeping fowler° eye,
    Or russet-pated choughs,° many in sort,
    Rising and cawing at the gun's report,
    Sever themselves and madly sweep the sky—
    So at this sight away his fellows fly,
25    And at our stamp here o'er and o'er one falls;
    He 'Murder!' cries, and help from Athens calls.
    Their sense thus weak, lost with their fears thus strong,

---

  9   **patches**  clowns
 17   **nole**  head
 20   **fowler**  bird hunter
 21   **russet-pated choughs**  grey-headed jackdaws

Made senseless things begin to do them wrong,
For briars and thorns at their apparel snatch,
30  Some sleeves, some hats; from yielders all things catch.
I led them on in this distracted fear,
And left sweet Pyramus translated there;
When in that moment, so it came to pass,
Titania waked, and straightway loved an ass.

35  **OBERON.**  This falls out better than I could devise.
But hast thou yet latched the Athenian's eyes
With the love juice, as I did bid thee do?

**PUCK.**  I took him sleeping—that is finished too—
And the Athenian woman by his side,
40  That when he waked, of force she must be eyed.

[*Enter DEMETRIUS and HERMIA.*]

**OBERON.**  Stand close: this is the same Athenian.

**PUCK.**  This is the woman, but not this the man.

**DEMETRIUS.**  O, why rebuke you him that loves you so?
Lay breath so bitter on your bitter foe.

45  **HERMIA.**  Now I but chide; but I should use thee worse,
For thou, I fear, hast given me cause to curse.
If thou hast slain Lysander in his sleep,
Being o'er shoes in blood, plunge in the deep,
And kill me too.
50  The sun was not so true unto the day
As he to me. Would he have stol'n away
From sleeping Hermia? I'll believe as soon
This whole earth may be bored, and that the moon
May through the centre creep, and so displease
55  Her brother's noontide with th'Antipodes.
It cannot be but thou hast murdered him·
So should a murderer look; so dead, so grim.

**DEMETRIUS.**  So should the murdered look, and so should I,
Pierced through the heart with your stern cruelty;
60  Yet you, the murderer, look as bright, as clear,
As yonder Venus in her glimmering sphere.

**HERMIA.**  What's this to my Lysander? Where is he?

Ah, good Demetrius, wilt thou give him me?

DEMETRIUS.   I had rather give his carcass to my hounds.

65  HERMIA.   Out, dog! Out, cur! Thou driv'st me past the bounds
Of maiden's patience. Hast thou slain him then?
Henceforth be never numbered among men.
O, once tell true; tell true, even for my sake:
Durst thou have looked upon him being awake?
70  And hast thou killed him sleeping? O, brave touch!
Could not a worm, an adder do so much?
An adder did it; for with doubler tongue
Than thine, thou serpent, never adder stung.

DEMETRIUS.   You spend your passion on a misprised mood,
75  I am not guilty of Lysander's blood,
Nor is he dead, for aught that I can tell.

HERMIA.   I pray thee, tell me then that he is well.

DEMETRIUS.   And if I could, what should I get therefor?

HERMIA.   A privilege, never to see me more;
80  And from thy hated presence part I so.
See me no more, whether he be dead or no.

[*Exit* HERMIA.]

DEMETRIUS.   There is no following her in this fierce vein;
Here therefore for a while I will remain.
So sorrow's heaviness doth heavier grow
85  For debt that bankrupt sleep doth sorrow owe,
Which now in some slight measure it will pay,
If for his tender here I make some stay.

[*He lies down and sleeps.*]

OBERON.   What hast thou done? Thou hast mistaken quite,
And laid the love juice on some true love's sight.
90  Of thy misprision° must perforce ensue
Some true love turned, and not a false turned true.

PUCK.   Then fate o'errules, that, one man holding troth,
A million fail, confounding oath on oath.

OBERON.   About the wood go swifter than the wind,
95  And Helena of Athens look thou find.

---

90   **misprision** mistake

All fancy-sick° she is and pale of cheer
With sighs of love, that costs the fresh blood dear.
By some illusion see thou bring her here;
I'll charm his eyes against she do appear.

100 **PUCK.** I go, I go, look how I go!
Swifter than arrow from the Tartar's° bow.

[*Exit PUCK.*]

**OBERON.** [*Squeezing the juice on DEMETRIUS' eyes.*]
Flower with this purple dye,
Hit with Cupid's archery,
Sink in apple of his eye.
105 When his love he doth espy,
Let her shine as gloriously
As the Venus of the sky.
When thou wak'st, if she be by,
Beg of her for remedy.

[*Enter PUCK.*]

110 **PUCK.** Captain of our fairy band,
Helena is here at hand,
And the youth mistook by me,
Pleading for a lover's fee.
Shall we their fond pageant see?
115 Lord, what fools these mortals be!

**OBERON.** Stand aside. The noise they make
Will cause Demetrius to awake.

**PUCK.** Then will two at once woo one—
That must needs be sport alone;
120 And those things do best please me
That befall prepost'rously.

[*Enter LYSANDER and HELENA.*]

**LYSANDER.** Why should you think that I should woo in scorn?
Scorn and derision never come in tears.
Look when I vow, I weep; and vows so born,
125 In their nativity all truth appears.
How can these things in me seem scorn to you,
Bearing the badge of faith to prove them true?

---

96   **fancy-sick**  sick with love
101   **Tartar**  Central Asian warrior

HELENA.   You do advance your cunning more and more.
　　　When truth kills truth, O devilish-holy fray!
130　These vows are Hermia's. Will you give her o'er?
　　　　Weigh oath with oath, and you will nothing weigh;
　　　Your vows to her and me, put in two scales,
　　　Will even weigh, and both as light as tales.

LYSANDER.   I had no judgement when to her I swore.

135　HELENA.   Nor none, in my mind, now you give her o'er.

LYSANDER.   Demetrius loves her, and he loves not you.

DEMETRIUS.   [*Waking.*]
　　　O Helen, goddess, nymph, perfect, divine!
　　　To what, my love, shall I compare thine eyne?
　　　Crystal is muddy! O, how ripe in show
140　Thy lips, those kissing cherries, tempting grow!
　　　That pure congealèd white, high Taurus'° snow,
　　　Fanned with the eastern wind, turns to a crow
　　　When thou hold'st up thy hand. O, let me kiss
　　　This princess of pure white, this seal of bliss!

145　HELENA.   O spite! O Hell! I see you all are bent
　　　To set against me for your merriment.
　　　If you were civil, and knew courtesy,
　　　You would not do me thus much injury.
　　　Can you not hate me, as I know you do,
150　But you must join in souls to mock me too?
　　　If you were men, as men you are in show,
　　　You would not use a gentle lady so,
　　　To vow, and swear, and superpraise my parts,
　　　When I am sure you hate me with your hearts.
155　You both are rivals, and love Hermia;
　　　And now both rivals to mock Helena.
　　　A trim exploit, a manly enterprise,
　　　To conjure tears up in a poor maid's eyes
　　　With your derision! None of noble sort
160　Would so offend a virgin, and extort
　　　A poor soul's patience, all to make you sport.

LYSANDER.   You are unkind, Demetrius: be not so,
　　　For you love Hermia—this you know I know—
　　　And here with all good will, with all my heart,

---

　　141　**Taurus** mountains in Turkey

165       In Hermia's love I yield you up my part;
        And yours of Helena to me bequeath,
        Whom I do love, and will do till my death.

**HELENA.**   Never did mockers waste more idle breath.

**DEMETRIUS.**   Lysander, keep thy Hermia; I will none.
170       If e'er I loved her, all that love is gone.
        My heart to her but as guest-wise sojourned,°
        And now to Helen is it home returned,
        There to remain.

**LYSANDER.**              Helen, it is not so.

**DEMETRIUS.**   Disparage not the faith thou dost not know,
175       Lest to thy peril thou aby° it dear.
        Look where thy love comes: yonder is thy dear.

[*Enter* HERMIA.]

**HERMIA.**   Dark night, that from the eye his function takes,
        The ear more quick of apprehension makes;
        Wherein it doth impair the seeing sense
180       It pays the hearing double recompense.
        Thou art not by mine eye, Lysander, found;
        Mine ear, I thank it, brought me to thy sound.
        But why unkindly didst thou leave me so?

**LYSANDER.**   Why should he stay whom love doth press to go?

185 **HERMIA.**   What lover could press Lysander from my side?

**LYSANDER.**   Lysander's love, that would not let him bide,
        Fair Helena—who more engilds° the night
        Than all yon fiery oes° and eyes of light.
        [*To* HERMIA.] Why seek'st thou me? Could not this make
          thee know
190       The hate I bare thee made me leave thee so?

**HERMIA.**   You speak not as you think; it cannot be.

**HELENA.**   Lo, she is one of this confederacy!°
        Now I perceive they have conjoined all three

---

171   **sojourned** traveled, stayed
175   **aby** pay
187   **engilds** brightens, makes golden
188   **oes** bright dress ornaments
192   **confederacy** plot

To fashion this false sport in spite of me.
195 Injurious Hermia, most ungrateful maid,
Have you conspired, have you with these contrived
To bait me with this foul derision?
Is all the counsel that we two have shared,
The sisters' vows, the hours that we have spent
200 When we have chid° the hasty-footed time
For parting us—O, is all forgot?
All schooldays' friendship, childhood innocence?
We, Hermia, like two artificial gods
Have with our needles created both one flower,
205 Both on one sampler,° sitting on one cushion,
Both warbling of one song, both in one key,
As if our hands, our sides, voices, and minds
Had been incorporate. So we grew together
Like to a double cherry, seeming parted,
210 But yet an union in partition,
Two lovely berries moulded on one stem;
So with two seeming bodies but one heart,
Two of the first, like coats in heraldry,
Due but to one, and crownèd with one crest.
215 And will you rent our ancient love asunder,
To join with men in scorning your poor friend?
It is not friendly, 'tis not maidenly.
Our sex, as well as I, may chide you for it,
Though I alone do feel the injury.

220 HERMIA.    I am amazèd at your passionate words.
I scorn you not; it seems that you scorn me.

HELENA.    Have you not set Lysander, as in scorn,
To follow me, and praise my eyes and face?
And made your other love, Demetrius,
225 Who even but now did spurn me with his foot,
To call me goddess, nymph, divine and rare,
Precious, celestial? Wherefore speaks he this
To her he hates? And wherefore doth Lysander
Deny your love, so rich within his soul,
230 And tender me, forsooth, affection,
But by your setting on, by your consent?

---

200    **chid**  scolded
205    **sampler**  piece of embroidery

What though I be not so in grace as you,
So hung upon with love, so fortunate,
But miserable most, to love unloved:
235  This you should pity rather than despise.

**HERMIA.**  I understand not what you mean by this.

**HELENA.**  Ay, do! Persever,° counterfeit sad looks,
Make mouths upon me when I turn my back,
Wink each at other, hold the sweet jest up.
240  This sport, well carried, shall be chronicled.
If you have any pity, grace, or manners,
You would not make me such an argument.
But fare ye well. 'Tis partly my own fault,
Which death or absence soon shall remedy.

245  **LYSANDER.**  Stay, gentle Helena: hear my excuse,
My love, my life, my soul, fair Helena!

**HELENA.**  O, excellent!

**HERMIA.**  [*To Lysander.*] Sweet, do not scorn her so.

**DEMETRIUS.**  If she cannot entreat, I can compel.

**LYSANDER.**  Thou canst compel no more than she entreat;
250  Thy threats have no more strength than her weak prayers.
Helen, I love thee, by my life, I do:
I swear by that which I will lose for thee
To prove him false that says I love thee not.

**DEMETRIUS.**  I say I love thee more than he can do.

255  **LYSANDER.**  If thou say so, withdraw, and prove it too.

**DEMETRIUS.**  Quick, come.

**HERMIA.**                          Lysander, whereto tends all this?

**LYSANDER.**  Away, you Ethiop!

**DEMETRIUS.**                          No, no sir,
Seem to break loose, take on as you would follow,
But yet come not. You are a tame man, go.

260  **LYSANDER.**  Hang off, thou cat, thou burr!° Vile thing, let loose,
Or I will shake thee from me like a serpent.

---

237  **persever**  persevere, continue
260  **burr**  prickly seed case of a plant

**HERMIA.** Why are you grown so rude? What change is this,
Sweet love?

**LYSANDER.**    Thy love?—out, tawny Tartar, out;
Out, loathed medicine! O hated potion, hence!

265 **HERMIA.** Do you not jest?

**HELENA.**                    Yes, sooth, and so do you.

**LYSANDER.** Demetrius, I will keep my word with thee.

**DEMETRIUS.** I would I had your bond, for I perceive
A weak bond holds you. I'll not trust your word.

**LYSANDER.** What? Should I hurt her, strike her, kill her dead?
270    Although I hate her, I'll not harm her so.

**HERMIA.** What? Can you do me greater harm than hate?
Hate me? Wherefore? O me, what news, my love?
Am not I Hermia? Are not you Lysander?
I am as fair now as I was erewhile.
275    Since night you loved me; yet since night you left me.
Why then, you left me—O, the gods forbid!—
In earnest, shall I say?

**LYSANDER.**                    Ay, by my life;
And never did desire to see thee more.
Therefore be out of hope, of question, of doubt;
280    Be certain, nothing truer—'tis no jest
That I do hate thee and love Helena.

**HERMIA.**    [*To Helena.*]
O me, you juggler, you canker-blossom,°
You thief of love! What, have you come by night
And stol'n my love's heart from him?

**HELENA.**                              Fine, i'faith!
285    Have you no modesty, no maiden shame,
No touch of bashfulness? What, will you tear
Impatient answers from my gentle tongue?
Fie, fie, you counterfeit, you puppet, you!

**HERMIA.**    'Puppet'? Why so?—Ay, that way goes the game.
290    Now I perceive that she hath made compare

---

282    **canker-blossom** diseased flower

Between our statures; she hath urged her height,
And with her personage, her tall personage,
Her height, forsooth, she hath prevailed with him.
And are you grown so high in his esteem
295 Because I am so dwarfish and so low?
How low am I, thou painted maypole? Speak!
How low am I? I am not yet so low
But that my nails can reach unto thine eyes.

HELENA. I pray you, though you mock me, gentlemen,
300 Let her not hurt me. I was never curst;
I have no gift at all in shrewishness.
I am a right maid for my cowardice;
Let her not strike me. You perhaps may think
Because she is something lower than myself
305 That I can match her.

HERMIA.                    Lower? Hark, again!

HELENA. Good Hermia, do not be so bitter with me.
I evermore did love you, Hermia,
Did ever keep your counsels, never wronged you,
Save that in love unto Demetrius
310 I told him of your stealth unto this wood.
He followed you; for love I followed him,
But he hath chid° me hence, and threatened me
To strike me, spurn me, nay, to kill me too.
And now, so you will let me quiet go,
315 To Athens will I bear my folly back,
And follow you no further. Let me go;
You see how simple and how fond I am.

HERMIA. Why, get you gone! Who is't that hinders you?

HELENA. A foolish heart that I leave here behind.

320 HERMIA. What, with Lysander?

HELENA.                              With Demetrius.

LYSANDER. Be not afraid; she shall not harm thee, Helena.

DEMETRIUS. No, sir. She shall not, though you take her part.

HELENA. O, when she is angry she is keen and shrewd;
She was a vixen when she went to school,

---

312 **chid** scolded

325     And though she be but little, she is fierce.

     **HERMIA.**    Little again? Nothing but low and little?
          Why will you suffer her to flout me thus?
          Let me come to her.

     **LYSANDER.**                    Get you gone, you dwarf,
          You minimus of hindering knot-grass° made,
330        You bead, you acorn.

     **DEMETRIUS.**                    You are too officious
          In her behalf that scorns your services.
          Let her alone: speak not of Helena,
          Take not her part; for if thou dost intend
          Never so little show of love to her,
335        Thou shalt aby° it.

     **LYSANDER.**                    Now she holds me not—
          Now follow, if thou dur'st, to try whose right,
          Of thine or mine, is most in Helena.

     **DEMETRIUS.**    Follow? Nay, I'll go with thee, cheek by jowl.

[*Exit* LYSANDER *and* DEMETRIUS.]

     **HERMIA.**    You, mistress, all this coil° is 'long° of you.
340        Nay, go not back.

     **HELENA.**                    I will not trust you, I,
          Nor longer stay in your curst company.
          Your hands than mine are quicker for a fray;°
          My legs are longer, though, to run away!

[*Exit* HELENA.]

     **HERMIA.**    I am amazed, and know not what to say.

[*Exit* HERMIA.]

[*OBERON and* PUCK *come forward.*]

345  **OBERON.**    This is thy negligence. Still thou mistak'st,
          Or else committ'st thy knaveries willfully.

     **PUCK.**    Believe me, King of Shadows, I mistook.

---

329   **knot-grass**  a weed which that was thought to stunt growth
335   **aby**  pay for
339   **coil**  turmoil
        **'long**  because of
342   **fray**  fight

Did not you tell me I should know the man
By the Athenian garments he had on?
350 And so far blameless proves my enterprise
That I have 'nointed an Athenian's eyes;
And so far am I glad it so did sort,
As this their jangling I esteem a sport.

**OBERON.** Thou seest these lovers seek a place to fight:
355 Hie therefore, Robin, overcast the night;
The starry welkin° cover thou anon
With drooping fog as black as Acheron,°
And lead these testy rivals so astray
As one come not within another's way.
360 Like to Lysander sometime frame thy tongue,
Then stir Demetrius up with bitter wrong,
And sometime rail° thou like Demetrius;
And from each other look thou lead them thus,
Till o'er their brows death-counterfeiting sleep
365 With leaden legs and batty wings doth creep.
Then crush this herb into Lysander's eye,
Whose liquor hath this virtuous property,
To take from thence all error with his might,
And make his eyeballs roll with wonted° sight.
370 When they next wake, all this derision
Shall seem a dream and fruitless vision,
And back to Athens shall the lovers wend
With league whose date till death shall never end.
Whiles I in this affair do thee employ
375 I'll to my Queen and beg her Indian boy;
And then I will her charmèd eye release
From monster's view, and all things shall be peace.

**PUCK.** My fairy lord, this must be done with haste,
For night's swift dragons cut the clouds full fast,
380 And yonder shines Aurora's harbinger,°
At whose approach ghosts wandering here and there
Troop home to churchyards. Damnèd spirits all,

---

356 **welkin** sky
357 **Acheron** one of the rivers in Hades, the underworld for the dead
362 **rail** use abusive language
369 **wonted** usual
380 **Aurora's harbinger** signal of the dawn—the morning star

That in crossways and floods have burial,
Already to their wormy beds are gone.
385   For fear lest day should look their shames upon,
They wilfully themselves exile from light,
And must for aye consort with black-browed night.

**OBERON.**   But we are spirits of another sort.
I with the morning's love have oft made sport,
390   And like a forester the groves may tread
Even till the eastern gate, all fiery-red,
Opening on Neptune° with fair blessèd beams,
Turns into yellow gold his salt green streams.
But notwithstanding, haste, make no delay;
395   We may effect this business yet ere day.

[*Exit* OBERON.]

**PUCK.**   Up and down, up and down,
I will lead them up and down;
I am feared in field and town.
Goblin, lead them up and down.
400   Here comes one.

[*Enter* LYSANDER.]

**LYSANDER.**   Where art thou, proud Demetrius? Speak thou now.

**PUCK.**   Here, villain, drawn and ready! Where art thou?

**LYSANDER.**   I will be with thee straight.

**PUCK.**                                         Follow me then
To plainer ground.

[*Exit* LYSANDER.]

[*Enter* DEMETRIUS.]

**DEMETRIUS.**            Lysander, speak again.
405   Thou runaway, thou coward, art thou fled?
Speak! In some bush? Where dost thou hide thy head?

**PUCK.**   Thou coward, art thou bragging to the stars,
Telling the bushes that thou look'st for wars,
And wilt not come? Come, recreant,° come, thou child,

---

392   **Neptune**  god of the sea. The morning's sunbeams turn the sea from green to
'yellow gold,' transforming it.

409   **recreant**  coward, villain

410    I'll whip thee with a rod. He is defiled
       That draws a sword on thee.

       **DEMETRIUS.**                    Yea, art thou there?

       **PUCK.**    Follow my voice. We'll try no manhood here.

[*Exit* PUCK *and* DEMETRIUS.]

[*Enter* LYSANDER.]

       **LYSANDER.**    He goes before me, and still dares me on;
       When I come where he calls, then he is gone.
415    The villain is much lighter-heeled than I;
       I followed fast, but faster he did fly,
       That fallen am I in dark uneven way,
       And here will rest me. [*Lies down.*] Come, thou gentle day,
       For if but once thou show me thy grey light
420    I'll find Demetrius and revenge this spite. [*Sleeps.*]

[*Enter* PUCK *and* DEMETRIUS.]

       **PUCK.**    Ho, ho, ho! Coward, why com'st thou not?

       **DEMETRIUS.**    Abide° me if thou dar'st, for well I wot°
       Thou runn'st before me, shifting every place,
       And dar'st not stand nor look me in the face.
425    Where art thou now?

       **PUCK.**                    Come hither; I am here.

       **DEMETRIUS.**    Nay then, thou mock'st me. Thou shalt buy this dear
       If ever I thy face by daylight see.
       Now, go thy way; faintness constraineth me
       To measure out my length on this cold bed.
430    By day's approach look to be visited. [*Sleeps.*]

[*Enter* HELENA.]

       **HELENA.**    O weary night, O long and tedious night,
                 Abate° thy hours, shine comforts from the east,
                 That I may back to Athens by daylight
                     From these that my poor company detest;
435    And sleep, that sometimes shuts up sorrow's eye,
       Steal me awhile from mine own company. [*Sleeps.*]

       **PUCK.**    Yet but three? Come one more,

---

    422    **Abide** face
           **wot** know
    432    **Abate** diminish, cut short

Two of both kinds makes up four.
Here she comes, curst and sad.
440        Cupid is a knavish lad
Thus to make poor females mad.

[*Enter* HERMIA.]

**HERMIA.**    Never so weary, never so in woe,
      Bedabbled with the dew, and torn with briars—
I can no further crawl, no further go;
445       My legs can keep no pace with my desires.
Here will I rest me till the break of day.
Heavens shield Lysander, if they mean a fray. [*Sleeps.*]

**PUCK.**    On the ground
Sleep sound.
450       I'll apply
To your eye,
   Gentle lover, remedy.
[*Squeezes the juice on* LYSANDER'S *eyes.*]
When thou wak'st,
Thou tak'st
455       True delight
In the sight
Of thy former lady's eye;
And the country proverb known,
That every man should take his own,
460       In your waking shall be shown.
     Jack shall have Jill,
     Naught shall go ill:
The man shall have his mare again, and all shall be well.

[*Exit* PUCK; *the lovers remain on stage, asleep.*]

# Act 4

## SCENE 1. The wood.

[*Enter* TITANIA, *Queen of Fairies, and* BOTTOM, *and* FAIRIES *including* PEASEBLOSSOM, COBWEB, *and* MUSTARDSEED; *and the King* OBERON *behind them.*]

**TITANIA.**   Come sit thee down upon this flowery bed
　　While I thy amiable cheeks do coy,°
　　And stick musk-roses in thy sleek smooth head,
　　And kiss thy fair large ears, my gentle joy.

5　**BOTTOM.**   Where's Peaseblossom?

**PEASEBLOSSOM.**   Ready.

**BOTTOM.**   Scratch my head, Peaseblossom. Where's Mounsieur Cobweb?

**COBWEB.**   Ready.

10　**BOTTOM.**   Mounsieur Cobweb, good Mounsieur, get you your weapons in your hand, and kill me a red-hipped humble-bee on the top of a thistle; and, good Mounsieur, bring me the honey-bag. Do not fret yourself too much in the action, Mounsieur; and, good Mounsieur, have a care the honey-bag break not; I would be loath
15　to have you overflown with a honey-bag, signior. Where's Mounsieur Mustardseed?

**MUSTARDSEED.**   Ready.

**BOTTOM.**   Give me your neaf,° Mounsieur Mustardseed. Pray you, leave your courtesy, good Mounsieur.

20　**MUSTARDSEED.**   What's your will?

---

　2　**coy** caress
　18　**neaf** fist

BOTTOM.    Nothing, good Mounsieur, but to help Cavalery°
Peaseblossom to scratch. I must to the barber's, Mounsieur, for
methinks I am marvellous hairy about the face. And I am such a
tender ass, if my hair do but tickle me, I must scratch.

25    TITANIA.    What, wilt thou hear some music, my sweet love?

BOTTOM.    I have a reasonable good ear in music. Let's have the tongs
and the bones.°

TITANIA.    Or say, sweet love, what thou desir'st to eat.

BOTTOM.    Truly, a peck of provender, I could munch your good dry oats.
30    Methinks I have a great desire to a bottle of hay. Good hay, sweet
hay hath no fellow.

TITANIA.    I have a venturous fairy that shall seek
The squirrel's hoard, and fetch thee new nuts.

BOTTOM.    I had rather have a handful or two of dried peas. But, I pray
35    you, let none of your people stir me; I have an exposition of° sleep
come upon me.

TITANIA.    Sleep thou, and I will wind thee in my arms.
Fairies be gone, and be all ways away.

[*Exit* FAIRIES.]

So doth the woodbine° the sweet honeysuckle
40    Gently entwist; the female ivy so
Enrings the barky fingers of the elm.
O, how I love thee! How I dote on thee!

[*They sleep.*]

[*Enter* PUCK. OBERON *comes forward.*]

OBERON.    Welcome, good Robin. Seest thou this sweet sight?
Her dotage now I do begin to pity;
45    For, meeting her of late behind the wood
Seeking sweet favours for this hateful fool,
I did upbraid her and fall out with her,
For she his hairy temples then had rounded
With coronet of fresh and fragrant flowers;
50    And that same dew, which sometime on the buds

---

21    **Cavalery** a gentleman (Bottom's mistake for 'cavalier')
26–7    **tongs . . . bones** simple musical instruments
35    **exposition of** another of Bottom's mistakes; surely he means disposition to?
39    **woodbine** bindweed

Was wont to swell like round and orient pearls,
Stood now within the pretty flowerets' eyes
Like tears that did their own disgrace bewail.
When I had at my pleasure taunted her,
55 And she in mild terms begged my patience,
I then did ask of her her changeling child,
Which straight she gave me, and her fairy sent
To bear him to my bower in Fairyland.
And now I have the boy, I will undo
60 This hateful imperfection of her eyes.
And, gentle Puck, take this transformèd scalp
From off the head of this Athenian swain,°
That, he awaking when the other do,
May all to Athens back again repair,
65 And think no more of this night's accidents
But as the fierce vexation of a dream.
But first I will release the Fairy Queen.
[*Squeezing a herb on* TITANIA'S *eyes.*]
    Be as thou wast wont to be;
    See as thou wast wont to see.
70     Dian's bud o'er Cupid's flower
    Hath such force and blessèd power.
Now, my Titania, wake you, my sweet Queen!

**TITANIA.** [*Starting up.*]
My Oberon, what visions I have seen!
Methought I was enamoured of an ass.

75 **OBERON.** There lies your love.

**TITANIA.**                How came these things to pass?
O, how mine eyes do loathe his visage now!

**OBERON.** Silence awhile: Robin, take off this head.
Titania, music call, and strike more dead
Than common sleep of all these five the sense.

80 **TITANIA.** Music, ho, music such as charmeth sleep!
[*Soft music plays.*]

**PUCK.** [*To Bottom, removing the ass's head.*]
Now, when thou wak'st, with thine own fool's eyes peep.

**OBERON.** Sound, music! Come, my Queen, take hands with me,
And rock the ground whereon these sleepers be.

---

**62**   **swain** lover

[*They dance*.]
Now thou and I are new in amity,
85  And will tomorrow midnight solemnly
Dance in Duke Theseus' house triumphantly,
And bless it to all fair prosperity.
There shall the pairs of faithful lovers be
Wedded, with Theseus, all in jollity.

90  **PUCK.**  Fairy King, attend, and mark:
I do hear the morning lark.

**OBERON.**  Then, my Queen, in silence sad,
Trip we after night's shade;
We the globe can compass soon,
95  Swifter than the wandering moon.

**TITANIA.**  Come, my lord, and in our flight
Tell me how it came this night
That I sleeping here was found
With these mortals on the ground.

[*Exit OBERON, TITANIA, and PUCK.*]

[*Wind horns. Enter THESEUS with HIPPOLYTA, EGEUS, and all his train.*]

100  **THESEUS.**  Go, one of you, find out the forester;
For now our observation is performed,
And since we have the vaward° of the day,
My love shall hear the music of my hounds.
Uncouple in the western valley; let them go:
105  Dispatch, I say, and find the forester.

[*Exit an Attendant.*]

We will, fair Queen, up to the mountain's top,
And mark the musical confusion
Of hounds and echo in conjunction.

**HIPPOLYTA.**  I was with Hercules° and Cadmus° once,
110  When in a wood of Crete they bayed the bear
With hounds of Sparta: never did I hear
Such gallant chiding; for besides the groves,
The skies, the fountains, every region near

---

102  **vaward**  early part
109  **Hercules**  mythical Greek hero, famed for his strength
**Cadmus**  mythical founder of Thebes

Seemed all one mutual cry. I never heard
115 So musical a discord, such sweet thunder.

THESEUS.    My hounds are bred out of the Spartan kind,
So flewed, so sanded;° and their heads are hung
With ears that sweep away the morning dew;
Crook-kneed, and dewlapped like Thessalian bulls;
120 Slow in pursuit, but matched in mouth like bells,
Each under each. A cry more tuneable
Was never hallooed to nor cheered with horn
In Crete, in Sparta, nor in Thessaly.
Judge when you hear. But soft, what nymphs are these?

125 EGEUS.    My lord, this is my daughter here asleep,
And this Lysander; this Demetrius is,
This Helena, old Nedar's Helena.
I wonder of their being here together.

THESEUS.    No doubt they rose up early to observe
130 The rite of May, and hearing our intent
Came here in grace of our solemnity.
But speak, Egeus; is not this the day
That Hermia should give answer of her choice?

EGEUS.    It is, my lord.

135 THESEUS.    Go, bid the huntsmen wake them with their horns.
[Shout within; wind horns; the lovers all start up.]
Good morrow, friends. Saint Valentine is past;
Begin these woodbirds but to couple° now?
[The lovers kneel.]

LYSANDER.    Pardon, my lord.

THESEUS.                              I pray you all, stand up.
I know you two are rival enemies:
140 How comes this gentle concord in the world,
That hatred is so far from jealousy
To sleep by hate, and fear no enmity?

LYSANDER.    My lord, I shall reply amazedly,
Half sleep, half waking; but as yet, I swear,
145 I cannot truly say how I came here.
But as I think (for truly would I speak)

---

117    **so flewed, so sanded**  with similar jowls and similar sandy coloring
137    **couple**  pair up

And now I do bethink me, so it is—
I came with Hermia hither. Our intent
Was to be gone from Athens, where we might
150     Without the peril of the Athenian law—

**EGEUS.**    Enough, enough, my lord; you have enough—
I beg the law, the law upon his head!
They would have stol'n away, they would, Demetrius,
Thereby to have defeated you and me,
155     You of your wife, and me of my consent,
Of my consent that she should be your wife.

**DEMETRIUS.**    My lord, fair Helen told me of their stealth,
Of this their purpose hither to this wood;
And I in fury hither followed them,
160     Fair Helena in fancy following me.
But, my good lord, I wot not by what power
(But some power it is), my love to Hermia,
Melted as the snow, seems to me now
As the remembrance of an idle gaud°
165     Which in my childhood I did dote upon;
And all the faith, the virtue of my heart,
The object and the pleasure of mine eye,
Is only Helena. To her, my lord,
Was I betrothed ere I saw Hermia;
170     But like a sickness did I loathe this food.
But, as in health come to my natural taste,
Now I do wish it, love it, long for it,
And will for evermore be true to it.

**THESEUS.**    Fair lovers, you are fortunately met.
175     Of this discourse we more will hear anon.
Egeus, I will overbear your will;°
For in the temple, by and by, with us
These couples shall eternally be knit.
And, for the morning now is something worn,
180     Our purposed hunting shall be set aside.
Away with us to Athens. Three and three,
We'll hold a feast in great solemnity.
Come, Hippolyta.

---

164    **idle gaud** worthless toy
176    **overbear your will** overrule your decision

[*Exit* THESEUS *with* HIPPOLYTA, EGEUS, *and his train.*]

185
**DEMETRIUS.** These things seem small and undistinguishable,
Like far-off mountains turnèd into clouds.

**HERMIA.** Methinks I see these things with parted eye,
When everything seems double.

**HELENA.** So methinks;
And I have found Demetrius, like a jewel,
Mine own, and not mine own.

**DEMETRIUS.** Are you sure
190
That we are awake? It seems to me
That yet we sleep, we dream. Do not you think
The Duke was here, and bid us follow him?

**HERMIA.** Yea, and my father.

**HELENA.** And Hippolyta.

**LYSANDER.** And he did bid us follow to the temple.

195
**DEMETRIUS.** Why, then, we are awake. Let's follow him,
And by the way let us recount our dreams.

[*Exit lovers.*]

[BOTTOM *wakes.*]

200

205

210
**BOTTOM.** When my cue comes, call me, and I will answer. My next is
'Most fair Pyramus'. Heigh ho! Peter Quince? Flute the bellows-
mender? Snout the tinker? Starveling? God's my life! Stolen hence
and left me asleep! I have had a most rare vision. I have had a dream,
past the wit of man to say what dream it was. Man is but an ass
if he go about to expound this dream. Methought I was—there is
no man can tell what. Methought I was—and methought I had—but
man is but a patched fool if he will offer to say what methought
I had. The eye of man hath not heard, the ear of man hath not seen,
man's hand is not able to taste, his tongue to conceive, nor his heart
to report what my dream was! I will get Peter Quince to write a
ballad of this dream; it shall be called 'Bottom's Dream', because
it hath no bottom; and I will sing it in the latter end of a play, before
the Duke. Peradventure, to make it the more gracious, I shall sing
it at her death.

[*Exit* BOTTOM.]

## SCENE 2. Athens.

[*Enter* QUINCE, FLUTE, SNOUT, *and* STARVELING.]

**QUINCE.** Have you sent to Bottom's house? Is he come home yet?

**STARVELING.** He cannot be heard of. Out of doubt he is transported.

**FLUTE.** If he come not, then the play is marred. It goes not forward. Doth it?

5 **QUINCE.** It is not possible. You have not a man in all Athens able to discharge Pyramus but he.

**FLUTE.** No, he hath simply the best wit of any handicraft man in Athens.

**QUINCE.** Yea, and the best person, too; and he is a very paramour for a sweet voice.

10 **FLUTE.** You must say 'paragon'. A paramour is (God bless us!) a thing of naught.°

[*Enter* SNUG *the joiner.*]

**SNUG.** Masters, the Duke is coming from the temple, and there is two or three lords and ladies more married. If our sport had gone forward, we had all been made men.°

15 **FLUTE.** O, sweet bully Bottom! Thus hath he lost sixpence a day during his life: he could not have 'scaped sixpence a day. And the Duke had not given him sixpence a day for playing Pyramus, I'll be hanged. He would have deserved it. Sixpence a day in Pyramus, or nothing.

[*Enter* BOTTOM.]

20 **BOTTOM.** Where are these lads? Where are these hearts?

**QUINCE.** Bottom! O most courageous day! O most happy hour!

**BOTTOM.** Masters, I am to discourse wonders—but ask me not what; for if I tell you, I am not true Athenian. I will tell you everything, right as it fell out.

25 **QUINCE.** Let us hear, sweet Bottom.

**BOTTOM.** Not a word of me. All that I will tell you is—that the Duke hath dined. Get your apparel together, good strings to your beards, new ribbons to your pumps: meet presently at the palace, every man look o'er his part. For the short and the long is, our play is preferred.

30 In any case, let Thisbe have clean linen; and let not him that plays

---

10–11   **paramour . . . thing of naught** a mistress and, to Flute, something immoral and wicked

14   **made men** our fortunes would be made

the lion pare his nails, for they shall hang out for the lion's claws. And, most dear actors, eat no onions nor garlic; for we are to utter sweet breath, and I do not doubt but to hear them say it is a sweet comedy. No more words. Away! Go, away!

[*Exit all.*]

# Act 5

## SCENE 1. Athens. THESEUS' Palace.

[*Enter THESEUS, HIPPOLYTA, PHILOSTRATE, Lords, and Attendants.*]

**HIPPOLYTA.** 'Tis strange, my Theseus, that these lovers speak of.

**THESEUS.** More strange than true. I never may believe
These antique fables, nor these fairy toys.°
Lovers and madmen have such seething brains,
5     Such shaping fantasies, that apprehend
More than cool reason ever comprehends.
The lunatic, the lover, and the poet
Are of imagination all compact:°
One sees more devils than vast hell can hold;
10     That is the madman. The lover, all as frantic,
Sees Helen's beauty in a brow of Egypt.
The poet's eye, in a fine frenzy rolling,
Doth glance from heaven to earth, from earth to heaven;
And as imagination bodies forth
15     The forms of things unknown, the poet's pen
Turns them to shapes, and gives to airy nothing
A local habitation and a name.
Such tricks hath strong imagination
That if it would but apprehend some joy,
20     It comprehends some bringer of that joy;
Or in the night, imagining some fear,
How easy is a bush supposed a bear?

**HIPPOLYTA.** But all the story of the night told over,
And all their minds transfigured so together,
25     More witnesseth than fancy's images,

---

3   **toys** tales
8   **compact** composed

And grows to something of great constancy;
But howsoever, strange and admirable.

[*Enter the lovers:* LYSANDER, DEMETRIUS, HERMIA, *and* HELENA.]

**THESEUS.**   Here come the lovers, full of joy and mirth.
Joy, gentle friends, joy and fresh days of love
30      Accompany your hearts!

**LYSANDER.**           More than to us
Wait in your royal walks, you board, your bed!

**THESEUS.**   Come now: what masques,° what dances shall we have
To wear away this long age of three hours
Between our after-supper and bedtime?
35      Where is our usual manager of mirth?
What revels are in hand? Is there no play
To ease the anguish of a torturing hour?
Call Philostrate.

**PHILOSTRATE.**     Here, mighty Theseus.

**THESEUS.**   Say, what abridgement° have you for this evening?
40      What masque, what music? How shall we beguile
The lazy time if not with some delight?

**PHILOSTRATE.**   [*Giving him a paper.*]
There is a brief° how many sports are ripe.
Make choice of which your highness will see first.

**THESEUS.**   [*Reading.*]
'This battle with the Centaurs, to be sung
45      By an Athenian eunuch to the harp'—
We'll none of that; that have I told my love
In glory of my kinsman, Hercules.
[*Reading.*] 'The riot of the tipsy Bacchanals,°
Tearing the Thracian singer in their rage'—
50      That is an old device, and it was played
When I from Thebes came last a conqueror.
[*Reading.*] 'The thrice three Muses° mourning for the death
Of learning, late deceased in beggary'—

---

32   **masques**  dances or entertainments where masks were worn

39   **abridgement**  pastime; to make time go quickly

42   **brief**  a summary

48   **tipsy Bacchanals**  drunken women (from Greek mythology)

52   **Muses**  goddesses of learning and art

That is some satire keen and critical,
55      Not sorting with a nuptial ceremony.
        [*Reading.*] 'A tedious brief scene of young Pyramus
        And his love Thisbe, very tragical mirth'—
        Merry and tragical? Tedious and brief?
        That is hot ice and wondrous strange snow!
60      How shall we find the concord of this discord?

PHILOSTRATE.    A play there is, my lord, some ten words long,
        Which is as 'brief' as I have known a play,
        But by ten words, my lord, it is too long,
        Which makes it 'tedious'. For in all the play
65      There is not one word apt, one player fitted.
        And 'tragical', my noble lord, it is,
        For Pyramus therein doth kill himself,
        Which when I saw rehearsed, I must confess,
        Made mine eyes water; but more 'merry' tears
70      The passion of loud laughter never shed.

THESEUS.    What are they that do play it?

PHILOSTRATE.    Hard-handed men that work in Athens here,
        Which never laboured in their minds till now:
        And now have toiled their unbreathed° memories
75      With this same play against your nuptial.

THESEUS.    And we will hear it.

PHILOSTRATE.                    No, my noble lord,
        It is not for you. I have heard it over,
        And it is nothing, nothing in the world,
        Unless you can find sport in their intents,
80      Extremely stretched, and conned° with cruel pain,
        To do you service.

THESEUS.                    I will hear that play;
        For never anything can be amiss
        When simpleness and duty tender it.
        Go bring them in; and take your places, ladies.

[*Exit* PHILOSTRATE.]

---

74    **unbreathed** unpractised
80    **conned** learnt

85 **HIPPOLYTA.**   I love not to see wretchedness o'ercharged,°
And duty in his service perishing.

**THESEUS.**   Why, gentle sweet, you shall see no such thing.

**HIPPOLYTA.**   He says they can do nothing in this kind.

**THESEUS.**   The kinder we, to give them thanks for nothing.
90 Our sport shall be to take what they mistake;
And what poor duty cannot do, noble respect
Takes it in might, not merit.°
Where I have come, great clerks have purposèd
To greet me with premeditated welcomes,
95 Where I have seen them shiver and look pale,
Make periods° in the midst of sentences,
Throttle their practised accent in their fears,
And in conclusion dumbly have broke off,
Not paying me a welcome. Trust me, sweet,
100 Out of this silence yet I picked a welcome,
And in the modesty of fearful duty
I read as much as from the rattling tongue
Of saucy and audacious eloquence.
Love, therefore, and tongue-tied simplicity
105 In least speak most, to my capacity.°

[*Enter* PHILOSTRATE.]

**PHILOSTRATE.**   So please your grace, the Prologue is addressed.°

**THESEUS.**   Let him approach.

[*Flourish of trumpets.*]

[*Enter* QUINCE *as Prologue.*]

**QUINCE.**   If we offend, it is with our good will.
      That you should think, we come not to offend,
110      But with good will. To show our simple skill,
      That is the true beginning of our end.
      Consider then, we come but in despite.
      We do not come as minding to content you,
      Our true intent is. All for your delight,

---

85   **wretchedness o'ercharged**  those of little ability overstretched
92   **in might, not merit**  accepts it given the ability of those that offer it
96   **periods**  stops
105  **capacity**  understanding
106  **addressed**  ready

115            We are not here. That you should here repent you,
               The actors are at hand; and by their show
               You shall know all that you are like to know.

**THESEUS.**   This fellow doth not stand upon points.°

**LYSANDER.**   He hath rid his prologue like a rough colt; he knows not
120     the stop.° A good moral, my lord; it is not enough to speak, but to
speak true.

**HIPPOLYTA.**   Indeed, he hath played on this prologue like a child on
a recorder—a sound, but not in government.°

**THESEUS.**   His speech was like a tangled chain, nothing impaired, but
125     all disordered. Who is next?

[*Enter with a Trumpeter before them (*BOTTOM *as) Pyramus, (*FLUTE *as) Thisbe,
(*SNOUT *as) Wall, (*STARVELING *as) Moonshine, and (*SNUG *as) Lion.*]

**QUINCE.**   [*as Prologue.*]
    Gentles, perchance you wonder at this show,
       But wonder on, till truth make all things plain.
       This man is Pyramus, if you would know;
         This beauteous lady Thisbe is, certain.
130       This man with lime and rough-cast doth present
         Wall, that vile wall which did these lovers sunder:
       And through Wall's chink, poor souls, they are content
         To whisper—at the which let no man wonder.
       This man with lanthorn, dog, and bush of thorn,
135         Presenteth Moonshine; for, if you will know,
       By moonshine did these lovers think no scorn
         To meet at Ninus' tomb, there, there to woo.
       This grisly beast, which Lion hight by name,
       The trusty Thisbe, coming first by night,
140       Did scare away, or rather did affright;
       And as she fled, her mantle she did fall,
         Which Lion vile with bloody mouth did stain.
       Anon comes Pyramus, sweet youth and tall,
         And finds his trusty Thisbe's mantle slain;
145       Whereat with blade, with bloody, blameful blade,
         He bravely broached his boiling bloody breast;

---

118    **stand upon points**  take notice of punctuation or detail
120    **stop**  a pun on full stop, and suddenly stopping a horse when riding
123    **in government**  under control

And Thisbe, tarrying in mulberry shade,
  His dagger drew, and died. For all the rest,
Let Lion, Moonshine, Wall, and lovers twain
150    At large discourse, while here they do remain.

[*Exit* QUINCE, BOTTOM, FLUTE, SNUG, *and* STARVELING.]

**THESEUS.**    I wonder if the lion be to speak?

**DEMETRIUS.**    No wonder, my lord; one lion may, when many asses do.

**SNOUT.**  [*as Wall.*]
In this same interlude° it doth befall
That I, one Snout by name, present a wall;
155    And such a wall as I would have you think
That had in it a crannied hole or chink,
Through which the lovers, Pyramus and Thisbe,
Did whisper often, very secretly.
This loam, this rough-cast, and this stone doth show
160    That I am that same wall; the truth is so.
And this the cranny is, right and sinister,
Through which the fearful lovers are to whisper.

**THESEUS.**    Would you desire lime and hair to speak better?

**DEMETRIUS.**    It is the wittiest partition that ever I heard discourse, my
165    lord.

[*Enter* BOTTOM *as Pyramus.*]

**THESEUS.**    Pyramus draws near the wall; silence!

**BOTTOM.**  [*as Pyramus.*]
O grim-looked night, O night with hue so black,
  O night which ever art when day is not!
O night, O night, alack, alack, alack,
170    I fear my Thisbe's promise is forgot!
And thou, O wall, O sweet, O lovely wall,
  That stand'st between her father's ground and mine,
Thou wall, O wall, O sweet and lovely wall,
  Show me thy chink, to blink through with mine eyne.
[*Wall parts his fingers.*]
175    Thanks, courteous wall; Jove shield thee well for this!
  But what see I? No Thisbe do I see.
O wicked wall, through whom I see no bliss,
  Cursed by thy stones for thus deceiving me!

---

153    **interlude** short play

**THESEUS.**    The wall, methinks, being sensible, should curse again.°

180  **BOTTOM.**    No, in truth sir, he should not. 'Deceiving me' is Thisbe's
cue. She is to enter now, and I am to spy her through the wall.
You shall see it will fall pat as I told you. Yonder she comes.

[*Enter FLUTE as Thisbe.*]

**FLUTE.**    [*as Thisbe.*]
O wall, full often hast thou heard my moans,
    For parting my fair Pyramus and me.
185     My cherry lips have often kissed thy stones,
    Thy stones with lime and hair knit up in thee.

**BOTTOM.**    [*as Pyramus.*]
I see a voice; now will I to the chink,
    To spy and I can hear my Thisbe's face.
Thisbe!

**FLUTE.**    [*as Thisbe.*]
        My love! Thou art my love, I think?

**BOTTOM.**    [*as Pyramus.*]
190     Think what thou wilt, I am thy lover's grace,
And like Limander° am I trusty still.

**FLUTE.**    [*as Thisbe.*]
And I like Helen,° till the Fates me kill.

**BOTTOM.**    [*as Pyramus.*]
Not Shafalus° to Procrus° was so true.

**FLUTE.**    [*as Thisbe.*]
As Shafalus to Procrus, I to you.

**BOTTOM.**    [*as Pyramus.*]
195     O, kiss me through the hole of this vile wall!

**FLUTE.**    [*as Thisbe.*]
I kiss the wall's hole, not your lips at all.

**BOTTOM.**    [*as Pyramus.*]
Wilt thou at Ninny's tomb meet me straightway?

**FLUTE.**    [*as Thisbe.*]
Tide° life, tide death, I come without delay.

---

179  **curse again**  should curse back, since it is 'sensible' (alive)
191-2  **Limander, Helen**  this should be Leander and Hero, two legendary lovers
193  **Shafalus, Procrus**  this should be Cephalus and Procris, other legendary lovers
198  **tide**  come

[*Exit* BOTTOM *and* FLUTE *in different directions.*]

SNOUT.  [*as Wall.*]
    Thus have I, Wall, my part dischargèd so;
200    And being done, thus Wall away doth go.

[*Exit* SNOUT.]

THESEUS.  Now is the mural° down between the two neighbours.

DEMETRIUS.  No remedy, my lord, when walls are so willful to hear without warning.

HIPPOLYTA.  This is the silliest stuff that ever I heard.

205  THESEUS.  The best in this kind are but shadows; and the worst are no worse, if imagination amend them.

HIPPOLYTA.  It must be your imagination then, and not theirs.

THESEUS.  If we imagine no worse of them than they of themselves, they may pass for excellent men. Here come two noble beasts in,
210  a man and a lion.

[*Enter (*SNUG *as*) Lion *and (*STARVELING *as*) Moonshine.*]

SNUG.  [*as Lion.*]
    You ladies, you whose gentle hearts do fear
      The smallest monstrous mouse that creeps on floor,
    May now, perchance, both quake and tremble here,
      When Lion rough in wildest rage doth roar.
215    Then know that I as Snug the joiner am
    A lion fell, nor else no lion's dam;
    For if I should as lion come in strife
    Into this place, 'twere pity on my life.

THESEUS.  A very gentle beast, and of a good conscience.

220  DEMETRIUS.  The very best at a beast, my lord, that e'er I saw.

LYSANDER.  This lion is a very fox for his valour.

THESEUS.  True; and a goose for his discretion.

DEMETRIUS.  Not so, my lord; for his valour cannot carry his discretion; and the fox carries the goose.°

---

201   **mural** wall

224   **fox . . . goose** the lion was supposed to be brave, the fox cunning (discretion), and the goose stupid

225     **THESEUS.** His discretion, I am sure, cannot carry his valour; for the goose carries not the fox. It is well: leave it to his discretion, and let us listen to the moon.

    **STARVELING.** [*as Moonshine.*]
    This lanthorn doth the hornèd moon present—

    **DEMETRIUS.** He should have worn the horns on his head.°

230     **THESEUS.** He is no crescent, and his horns are invisible within the circumference.

    **STARVELING.** [*as Moonshine.*]
    This lanthorn doth the hornèd moon present;
      Myself the man i'th'moon do seem to be—

    **THESEUS.** This is the greatest error of all the rest; the man should be
235     put into the lantern. How is it else the man i'th'moon?

    **DEMETRIUS.** He dares not come there, for the candle; for you see it is already in snuff.

    **HIPPOLYTA.** I am aweary of this moon. Would he would change!

    **THESEUS.** It appears by his small light of discretion that he is in the
240     wane; but yet in courtesy, in all reason, we must stay the time.

    **LYSANDER.** Proceed, Moon.

    **STARVELING.** All that I have to say is to tell you that the lanthorn is the moon, I the man i'th'moon, this thorn bush my thorn bush, and this dog my dog.

245     **DEMETRIUS.** Why, all these should be in the lantern, for all these are in the moon. But silence; here comes Thisbe.

[*Enter (FLUTE as) Thisbe.*]

    **FLUTE.** [*as Thisbe.*]
    This is old Ninny's tomb. Where is my love?

    **SNUG.** [*as Lion.*] O!
    [*Lion roars. Thisbe runs off (dropping her mantle).*]

    **DEMETRIUS.** Well roared, Lion!

250     **THESEUS.** Well run, Thisbe!

    **HIPPOLYTA.** Well shone, Moon! Truly, the moon shines with a good grace.

---

229   **horns on his head** the sign of a cuckold (someone whose wife has been unfaithful)

**THESEUS.**   Well moused,° Lion!

**DEMETRIUS.**   And then came Pyramus—

255   **LYSANDER.**   And so the lion vanished.

[*Lion worries Thisbe's mantle, and exit.*]

[*Enter* BOTTOM *as Pyramus.*]

    **BOTTOM.**   [*as Pyramus.*]
      Sweet moon, I thank thee for thy sunny beams;
        I thank thee, moon, for shining now so bright;
      For by thy gracious, golden, glittering gleams
        I trust to take of truest Thisbe sight.
260                But stay—O spite!
             But mark, poor Knight,
      What dreadful dole is here?
          Eyes, do you see?
          How can it be?
265         O dainty duck, O dear!
          Thy mantle good—
          What, stained with blood?
      Approach, ye Furies fell!
          O Fates,° come, come,
270             Cut thread and thrum,°
      Quail, crush, conclude, and quell.

    **THESEUS.**   This passion, and the death of a dear friend, would go near
    to make a man look sad.

    **HIPPOLYTA.**   Beshrew my heart,° but I pity the man.

    **BOTTOM.**   [*as Pyramus.*]
275       O wherefore, Nature, didst thou lions frame,
      Since lion vile hath here deflowered my dear?
    Which is—no, no—which was the fairest dame
      That lived, that loved, that liked, that looked with cheer.
        Come tears, confound!
280           Out sword, and wound
      The pap° of Pyramus,
        Ay, that left pap,

---

  253   **well moused**  the lion is like a cat with a mouse (the mantle)

139-70   **Fates, thread and thrum**  the goddesses controlling lives, spinning out the threads of people's
    lives, and ending them by cutting the thread (and thrum)

  274   **beshrew my heart**  exclamation, like 'Bless my soul!'

  281   **pap**  breast

Where heart doth hop:
Thus die I, thus, thus, thus! [*Stabs himself.*]
285     Now am I dead,
Now am I fled:
My soul is in the sky.
Tongue lose thy light;
Moon, take thy flight;

[*Exit* STARVELING.]

290     Now die, die, die, die, die. [*He dies.*]

DEMETRIUS.    No die,° but an ace for him; for he is but one.

LYSANDER.    Less than an ace, man; for he is dead, he is nothing.

THESEUS.    With the help of a surgeon he might yet recover, and yet
prove an ass.

295     HIPPOLYTA.    How chance Moonshine is gone before Thisbe comes
back and finds her lover?

THESEUS.    She will find him by starlight.

[*Enter (*FLUTE *as*) *Thisbe.*]

Here she comes and her passion ends the play.

HIPPOLYTA.    Methinks she should not use a long one for such a
300     Pyramus; I hope she will be brief.

DEMETRIUS.    A mote° will turn the balance, which Pyramus, which
Thisbe is the better: he for a man, God warrant us; she for a woman,
God bless us.

LYSANDER.    She hath spied him already, with those sweet eyes.

305     DEMETRIUS.    And thus she means, videlicet—°

FLUTE.    [*as Thisbe.*]
Asleep, my love?
What, dead, my dove?
O Pyramus, arise.
Speak, speak! Quite dumb?
310     Dead, dead? A tomb
Must cover thy sweet eyes.

---

291     **die**  one of a pair of dice; an ace (one) is the lowest throw (Demetrius puns on Bottom's use
of 'die')

301     **mote**  minute particle

305     **means, videlicet**  moans, makes a formal legal complaint

These lily lips,
This cherry nose,
These yellow cowslip cheeks
315                    Are gone, are gone.
Lovers, make moan;
His eyes were green as leeks.
O sisters three,°
Come, come to me
320                    With hands as pale as milk;
Lay them in gore,°
Since you have shore°
With shears his thread of silk.
Tongue, not a word!
325                    Come, trusty sword,
Come blade, my breast imbrue!° [*Stabs herself.*]
And farewell, friends.
Thus Thisbe ends—
Adieu, adieu, adieu! [*Dies.*]

330    **THESEUS.**    Moonshine and Lion are left to bury the dead.

        **DEMETRIUS.**    Ay, and Wall, too.

        **BOTTOM.**    [*Starting up, as FLUTE does also.*] No, I assure you, the wall
        is down that parted their fathers. Will it please you to see the
        epilogue, or to hear a Bergomask° dance between two of our
        company?

335    **THESEUS.**    No epilogue, I pray you; for your play needs no excuse.
        Never excuse; for when the players are all dead, there need none to
        be blamed. Marry, if he that writ it had played Pyramus and
        hanged himself in Thisbe's garter, it would have been a fine
        tragedy: and so it is, truly, and very notably discharged. But come,
340    your Bergomask; let your epilogue alone.

        [*The company return; two of them dance, then exit BOTTOM, FLUTE,
        and their fellows.*]
        The iron tongue of midnight hath told° twelve.

---

318    **sisters three**  the Fates
321    **gore**  blood
322    **shore**  cut
326    **imbrue**  stab
334    **Bergomask**  a country dance
341    **iron-tongue ... told**  the bell has struck

Lovers, to bed; 'tis almost fairy time.
I fear we shall outsleep the coming morn
As much as we this night have overwatched.
345  This palpable-gross° play hath well beguiled
The heavy gait° of night. Sweet friends, to bed.
A fortnight hold we this solemnity
In nightly revels and new jollity.

[*They exit.*]

[*Enter* PUCK (*carrying a broom*).]

PUCK.  Now the hungry lion roars,
350        And the wolf behowls the moon,
Whilst the heavy ploughman snores,
  All with wary task foredone.°
Now the wasted brands° do glow,
  Whilst the screech-owl, screeching loud,
355  Puts the wretch that lies in woe
  In remembrance of a shroud.
Now it is the time of night
  That the graves, all gaping wide,
Every one lets forth his sprite
360    In the church-way paths to glide.
And we fairies, that do run
  By the triple Hecate's team°
From the presence of the sun,
  Following darkness like a dream,
365  Now are frolic; not a mouse
Shall disturb this hallowed house.
I am sent with broom before
To sweep the dust behind the door.

[*Enter* OBERON *and* TITANIA, *the King and Queen of Fairies, with all their train.*]

OBERON.  Through the house give glimmering light
370        By the dead and drowsy fire;

---

345  **palpable-gross**  uncouth
346  **heavy gait**  labored passage, slow-moving pace
352  **foredone**  worn out
353  **wasted brands**  burnt logs
362  **triple Hecate's team**  the moon's chariot

Every elf and fairy sprite
    Hop as light as bird from briar,
And this ditty after me
Sing, and dance it trippingly.

375   **TITANIA.**   First rehearse your song by rote,
To each word a warbling note;
Hand in hand with fairy grace
Will we sing and bless this place.
*[Song and dance.]*

    **OBERON.**   Now until the break of day
380   Through this house each fairy stray.
To the best bride-bed will we,
Which by us shall blessèd be;
And the issue there create
Ever shall be fortunate.
385   So shall all the couples three
Ever true in loving be,
And the blots of nature's hand
Shall not in their issue stand.
Never mole, harelip, nor scar,
390   Nor mark prodigious,° such as are
Despisèd in nativity,
Shall upon their children be.
With this field-dew consecrate,
Every fairy take his gait,°
395   And each several chamber bless
Through this palace with sweet peace;
And the owner of it blessed
Ever shall in safety rest.
Trip away, make no stay;
400   Meet me all by break of day.

*[Exit all but PUCK.]*

    **PUCK.**   *[To the audience.]*
If we shadows have offended,
Think but this, and all is mended:
That you have but slumbered here
While these visions did appear;

---

390   **mark prodigious** birthmark that is ominous
394   **take his gait** go his way

405             And this weak and idle theme,
                    No more yielding but a dream,
                    Gentles, do not reprehend;
                    If you pardon, we will mend,
                    And, as I am an honest Puck,
410             If we have unearnèd luck
                    Now to 'scape the serpent's tongue
                    We will make amends ere long,
                    Else the Puck a liar call.
                    So, good night unto you all.
415             Give me your hands, if we be friends,
                    And Robin shall restore amends.°

[*Exit* PUCK.]

---

416     **restore amends** Puck will, in return, make amends

# Related Readings

# Comedy

**Christopher Fry**

*Christopher Fry's article was originally published in a 1951 issue of* Vogue *magazine. In the article, Fry discusses the fine line that separates comedy from tragedy and the way by which comedy leads readers to a new understanding of life. As you read this article, think about the elements that keep* A Midsummer Night's Dream *from becoming a tragedy and, instead, make it a comedy.*

A FRIEND ONCE TOLD ME that when he was under the influence of ether he dreamed he was turning over the pages of a great book, in which he knew he would find, on the last page, the meaning of life. The pages of the book were alternately tragic and comic, and he turned page after page, his excitement growing, not only because he was approaching the answer but because he couldn't know, until he arrived, on which side of the book the final page would be. At last it came: the universe opened up to him in a hundred words: and they were uproariously funny. He came back to consciousness crying with laughter, remembering everything. He opened his lips to speak. It was then, that the great and comic answer plunged back out of his reach.

If I had to draw a picture of the person of Comedy, it is so I should like to draw it: the tears of laughter running down the face, one hand still lying on the tragic page which so nearly contained the answer, the lips about to frame the great revelation, only to find it had gone as disconcertingly[1] as a chair twitched away when we went to sit down. Comedy is an escape, not from truth but from despair: a narrow escape into faith. It believes in a universal cause for delight, even though knowledge of the cause is always twitched away from under us, which leaves us to rest on our own buoyancy.[2] In tragedy every moment is eternity; in comedy eternity is a moment. In tragedy we suffer pain; in comedy pain is a fool, suffered gladly.

Charles Williams once said to me—indeed it was the last thing he said to me: he died not long after: and it was shouted from the tailboard of a moving bus, over the heads of pedestrians and bicyclists outside the Midland Station,

---

1. **disconcertingly** in a manner throwing one into confusion; perplexingly
2. **buoyancy** floating ability

Oxford—"When we're dead we shall have the sensation of having enjoyed life altogether, whatever has happened to us." The distance between us widened, and he leaned out into the space so that his voice should reach me: "Even if we've been murdered, what a pleasure to have been capable of it!"; and, having spoken the words for comedy, away he went like the revelation which almost came out of the ether.

He was not at all saying that everything is for the best in the best of all possible worlds. He was saying—or so it seems to me—that there is an angle of experience where the dark is distilled[3] into light: either here or hereafter, in or out of time: where our tragic fate finds itself with perfect pitch, and goes straight to the key which creation was composed in. And comedy senses and reaches out to this experience. It says, in effect, that, groaning as we may be, we move in the figure of a dance, and, so moving, we trace the outline of the mystery.

Laughter did not come by chance, but how or why it came is beyond comprehension, unless we think of it as a kind of perception.[4] The human animal, beginning to feel his spiritual inches, broke in on to an unfamiliar tension of life, where laughter became inevitable. But how? Could he, in his first unlaughing condition, have contrived[5] a comic view of life and then developed the strange rib-shaking response? Or is it not more likely that when he was able to grasp the tragic nature of time he was of a stature[6] to sense its comic nature also; and, by the experience of tragedy and the intuition of comedy, to make his difficult way. The difference between tragedy and comedy is the difference between experience and intuition. In the experience we strive against every condition of our animal life: against death, against the frustration of ambition, against the instability of human love. In the intuition we trust the arduous[7] eccentricities[8] we're born to, and see the oddness of a creature who has never got acclimatized[9] to being created. Laughter inclines me to know that man is essential spirit; his body, with its functions and accidents and frustrations, is endlessly quaint and remarkable to him; and though comedy accepts our position in time, it barely accepts our posture in space.

---

3. **distilled** condensed; purified

4. **perception** awareness

5. **contrived** invented; cleverly planned

6. **stature** degree of development

7. **arduous** difficult; troublesome

8. **eccentricities** peculiarities

9. **acclimatized** used to

The bridge by which we cross from tragedy to comedy and back again is precarious[10] and narrow. We find ourselves in one or the other by the turn of a thought; a turn such as we make when we turn from speaking to listening. I know that when I set about writing a comedy the idea presents itself to me first of all as tragedy. The characters press on to the theme with all their divisions and perplexities[11] heavy about them; they are already entered for the race to doom, and good and evil are an infernal[12] tangle skinning the fingers that try to unravel them. If the characters were not qualified for tragedy there would be no comedy, and to some extent I have to cross the one before I can light on the other. In a century less flayed[13] and quivering we might reach it more directly; but not now, unless every word we write is going to mock us. A bridge has to be crossed, a thought has to be turned. Somehow the characters have to unmortify[14] themselves: to affirm[15] life and assimilate[16] death and persevere in joy. Their hearts must be as determined as the phoenix;[17] what burns must also light and renew: not by a vulnerable[18] optimism but by a hard-won maturity of delight, by the intuition of comedy, an active patience declaring the solvency[19] of good. The Book of Job is the great reservoir of comedy. "But there is a spirit in a man . . . Fair weather cometh out of the north . . . The blessing of him that was ready to perish came upon me: And I caused the widow's heart to sing for joy."

I have come, you may think, to the verge[20] of saying that comedy is greater than tragedy. On the verge I stand and go no further. Tragedy's experience hammers against the mystery to make a breach[21] which would admit the whole triumphant answer. Intuition has no such potential. But there are times in the state of man when comedy has a special worth, and the present is one of them: a time when the loudest faith has been faith in a trampling materialism,[22] when literature has been thought unrealistic which did not mark and remark our poverty and doom. Joy (of a kind) has been all on the devil's side, and one of

---

10. **precarious** shaky
11. **perplexities** uncertainties
12. **infernal** hell-like
13. **flayed** beaten
14. **unmortify** become unashamed of
15. **affirm** confirm
16. **assimilate** absorb
17. **phoenix** mythical bird that rose from ashes; a symbol of renewal
18. **vulnerable** powerless; unguarded
19. **solvency** reliability
20. **verge** edge
21. **breach** opening
22. **materialism** love of things

the necessities of our time is to redeem it. If not, we are in poor sort to meet the circumstances, the circumstances being the contention of death with life, which is to say evil with good, which is to say desolation with delight. Laughter may seem to be only like an exhalation[23] of air, but out of that air we came; in the beginning we inhaled it; it is a truth, not a fantasy, a truth voluble[24] of good which comedy stoutly maintains.

---

23. **exhalation** breathing out
24. **voluble** flowing with words

**Norrie Epstein**

# Forget the Footnotes! And Other Advice

from
## *The Friendly Shakespeare*

*People are often intimidated by Shakespeare and his plays.
They feel that the plays are too difficult to understand and
thus avoid them altogether. In this short chapter of her
book, Norrie Epstein provides a variety of recommen-
dations from different experts on how to approach a
Shakespearean play.*

SOME EXPERTS ADVISE not to start reading Shakespeare until you're at
least sixty-five; others say the sooner the better. Some suggest reading the
plays before seeing them; others suggest seeing them first. To read footnotes,
or not to? And so on. People tend to procrastinate[1] because they think
there's a right way of "doing" Shakespeare. But just plunge in. See a play,
read it aloud, rent a video, listen to a tape. It's up to you. When you look at
Shakespeare close up, he's not as intimidating as when he's seen from afar.

To help you get started, experts offer the following suggestions:

The worst way of interpreting Shakespeare is to say he meant this,
and just this, and to give a formula. As David Hare said, "Shakespeare
was thinking while he was working through the plot," and this is the

---

1. **procrastinate** put off; wait

right way to approach Shakespeare. . . . But don't ask for simple answers from Shakespeare! Just believe in Shakespeare—in his greatness, in his wide outlook, in his ability to put into one play a whole world with all its contradictions, contrasts, and problems.

**Alexander Anikst**

First of all, you should read the play aloud. Don't read one scene today and then another tomorrow. It doesn't work that way. Read a whole scene without looking anything up. You'll be surprised by how much you know. We tend to fall into the trap of looking at every single footnote, and then we start looking at footnotes of words that we know, words like "ye" and "thee."

If there's a production near you, see it. If you're bored at the halfway point, leave. But don't blame Shakespeare for that production. Don't think that because you're bored, he's boring.

**Michael Tolaydo**

Listen to Shakespeare and don't listen to the critics. You don't need to understand every word, and if you don't, you can go back to the footnotes later.

**Louis Marder**

Don't read the play; see it first. It was Olivier's[2] *Henry V* that made me realize that Shakespeare was about real people and that his language wasn't simply beautiful poetry, but that it carried the vein of action. So I would advise someone to see the Branagh[3] and Olivier *Henrys*—or even the Olivier *Hamlet*, which is actually not all that good.

**Robert Brustein**

My advice to anybody going to the theatre: don't worry too much. Just make sure your ears are clean and your eyes are sharp. Listen and look and watch. Look at the distances people stand from each other; look at the relationships being developed. Don't be put off if during the first ten minutes you can't understand what's being said. Stay with it. Don't negate[4] the move that Shakespeare will make toward your gut, toward your soul— because he *will* touch you there, if you allow yourself to be touched.

**David Suchet**

---

2. **Olivier**  Laurence Olivier produced, directed, and starred in both *Henry V* in 1944 and *Hamlet* in 1948.

3. **Branagh**  Kenneth Branagh directed and starred in a 1989 version of *Henry V*.

4. **negate**  deny

Don't choose something you already did in school. *Othello* would be a good place to begin because it has only one plot to deal with. And it really moves: in the first eighty-five lines it's already going a hundred miles a hour. It's also very gripping. It has the parent-child theme, the racial issue, and there's Iago! There are a lot of adult emotions in the play. *Hamlet* can wait.

**Peggy O'Brien**

There are some parts of the plays you'll never understand. But excuse me, I thought that's what great art was supposed to be about. Don't freak out over it. . . . Keep reading.

**Peter Sellars**

## Academics versus Actors

But you don't have to choose between literary analysis[5] or theatrical representation. Each complements the other. Most non-Shakespeareans tend to imagine the Shakespeare scholar as Charles Dickens's Mr. Curdle, with his "pamphlet of sixty-four pages . . . on the character of the Nurse's deceased husband in *Romeo and Juliet.*" Such scholarship tends to wither the flesh-and-blood vitality of drama, which, after all, is meant to be enjoyed, not probed to death. But a play is also a text, and in the hands of a gifted teacher and critic it can be suddenly illuminated, revealing unsuspected and surprising meanings. For some scholars, the plays are dramatic poems, and what excites them is not necessarily the human situation the plays depict,[6] but Shakespeare's subtle use of language and how one word or image resonates[7] throughout a play and reflects its underlying meaning. Professors devote years to studying one image in *Hamlet* which a director might cut or an actor ignore. Linguistic analysis[8] reveals that in addition to being a powerful dramatist, Shakespeare was also a very great poet. As an example of how Shakespeare "unpacks" a word, allowing its various meanings to resonate throughout a play, Professor Marjorie Garber of Harvard University cites[9] the significance of ear imagery and poison in *Hamlet*—images that might be lost on a modern audience. (Claudius kills old King Hamlet by pouring poison in his ear.) "You can trace the poison metaphor or ear imagery throughout the play. Then think of all the spying and the eavesdropping that goes on in *Hamlet*. Or the way in which words can poison the listener." This is only one example, but in all of Shakespeare's

---

5. **literary analysis** the study of literature

6. **depict** represent

7. **resonates** echoes

8. **linguistic analysis** the study of the language

9. **cites** mentions especially

mature plays he rarely uses an idea or an image in isolation, but allows it to accumulate meaning, gathering depth and richness, so that a play is not just plot with events, but a unified work of art in which language, themes, and plot are woven together.

You can't get a sense of anything when you just read a play because you can't see the character who is on stage but who doesn't speak. For instance, you won't be able to understand Antonio in *The Merchant of Venice* because in that play Shakespeare created a dramatic situation where the main character rarely speaks. Get another person to be the silent character while you read a part aloud, and you'll discover why and what's being said.

**Tony Church**

The bastion[10] that protects William Shakespeare has been established by scholars, critics, teachers, litterateurs[11]—people with a vested[12] interest in language and the furtherance[13] of a literary tradition. It's in their interest that the texts remain sacrosanct[14]—that they're handed down from generation to generation, each providing new insights and new refinements like so many new glosses on an old painting. A process which, judging from the past two hundred years, can go on for at least another five hundred because there will never be a shortage of scholars to point out the semiotic[15] significance of the ass's head in *A Midsummer Night's Dream* or the tallow candle in *Macbeth* or the implications of the syllabus[16] of Wittenberg during the years Hamlet was supposed to have been enrolled there.

**Charles Marowitz**

The video series *Playing Shakespeare* is a superb introduction to the study of Shakespeare. Actors such as Patrick Stewart, Ben Kingsley, David Suchet, and Ian McKellen illustrate rather than talk about the essence of Shakespeare. The series demystifies Shakespeare, because instead of having an eminent professor hold forth and tell viewers what to think, it depicts

---

10. **bastion** fortress
11. **litterateurs** writers of literature
12. **vested** fixed
13. **furtherance** advancement
14. **sacrosanct** very sacred
15. **semiotic** symbolic, referring specifically to words
16. **syllabus** course of study

actors in a casual workshop setting grappling with[17] and arguing about various interpretations.

If you can't see a play or rent a video, you can always buy an audiocassette of any play. They are inexpensive, easy to listen to, and available at most record stores.

## To Read or to See the Plays?

The printed word can't convey the undertone and nuances[18] of speech. For that, you need to hear a gifted actor. Inflection[19] reveals at once whether a speaker is ironic, genuine, sad, or funny. Irony, for instance, is mainly conveyed through inflection and facial expression. Take that masterpiece of political irony, Marc Antony's funeral speech. To the novice,[20] "But Brutus is an honorable man" seems pretty straightforward. But when you *hear* the lines, an entirely new meaning emerges. What we hear is not a superficial bit of flattery or an honest assessment, but a brilliant stroke of rhetoric[21] in which Antony means precisely the reverse of what he says.

On the other hand, reading a play alone allows you to proceed at your own pace, giving you the time to dwell on poetry and the complex images that might fly right by you if they were only heard.

---

17. **grappling with** trying to understand
18. **nuances** subtle variations in tone
19. **inflection** voice variation
20. **novice** beginner
21. **rhetoric** effective use of speech or writing

**Victoria McKee**

# Based on an original idea by William Shakespeare

as published in *The Independent*, April 20, 1996

*After a rash of 1990s movies based on plays by Shakespeare, Victoria McKee explores the reasons for the renewed interest in the famous playwright. McKee talks to directors and actors such as Kenneth Branagh and Ian McKellen, and offers a brief history of Shakespeare in the movies.*

HOLLYWOOD HAS DISCOVERED a promising new scriptwriter who doesn't demand mega-millions for a screenplay or throw artistic temper tantrums when his words are cut or meddled with. And his work not only guarantees an audience but attracts many of the world's leading actors for well below their usual scale of fee. Now that Hollywood's twigged[1] that the Bard can be box office, everybody is getting in on the act. . . .

"Money's at the bottom of it," says Professor Stanley Wells, Director of the Shakespeare Institute of the University of Birmingham, and co-editor of *Shakespeare and the Moving Image*. "They've discovered Shakespeare can be good box office, which is equally connected with the willingness of certain big box office draws to appear in Shakespeare."

But there is now more Shakespeare on the screen than at any time since the golden age of the Forties and Fifties. [Actor] Ian McKellen [*Richard III*,

---

1. **twigged** noticed

1996] thinks the sudden surge of Hollywood Shakespeare is "basically because the BBC[2] and ITV[3] don't do Shakespeare anymore. If the BBC had agreed to finance *Richard III* we'd have done it for television. But they didn't, so we had to go to the U. S. for funding."

One of the strings usually attached to such backing is the stipulation[4] that some big American box office names take part, and the film inevitably opens first in the U. S. (in the autumn to be eligible for the next year's Oscars). For *Richard III* the American names were Annette Bening and Robert Downey Jr., who were encouraged to keep their accents to play the social-climbing Queen Elizabeth as a kind of Wallis Simpson and her brother as someone who was "Earl" by name, not by title.

"Hollywood has discovered that they can do these prestigious[5] Shakespeare projects for comparatively little, since people want to be in them," says McKellen, who waived[6] his own fee for a year out of dedication to the project that has . . . turned him into a Hollywood film star at last. Directed by Richard Loncraine, with McKellen adapting the screenplay from his Royal National Theatre performance directed by Richard Eyre, it cost a mere £6 million. Branagh's . . . *Hamlet* [had] a budget of about £12 million from the American company Castle Rock Films. Despite this he . . . managed to attract the likes of Charlton Heston, Robin Williams, Billy Crystal, Gerard Depardieu and Ken Dodd in cameo roles, in addition to all-star principals such as Julie Christie and Derek Jacobi.

"Actors are often glad of the opportunity to work in a film like this for much less money than they might otherwise command—for all the old cliches, that they are very good parts," says Branagh. The parts attract Hollywood actors, and the Hollywood actors attract audiences who would not be seen dead (though perhaps snoring loudly) in a theatre. Franco Zeffirelli's 1990 *Hamlet* is more likely to have brought a whole new audience to Shakespeare than to its star, Mel Gibson. "There is now less feeling that these plays can be tackled only by English actors with an enormous amount of Shakespeare experience," says Professor Wells, ". . . that a Mel Gibson can be trusted with Hamlet, or a Laurence Fishburne with Othello." The scholarly Wells is not perturbed at the thought of a Pulp Macbeth from Quentin Tarantino. "There has been an alternative series of films for a long time, the most notable Derek Jarman's *The Tempest* with

---

2. **BBC**  British Broadcasting Corporation
3. **ITV**  Information Television Network
4. **stipulation**  condition agreed upon
5. **prestigious**  valued; highly regarded
6. **waived**  gave up

Toyah Wilcox as Miranda. But they have usually been on low budgets and 'highbrow'[7] in the sense that most avant-garde[8] cinema tends to be."

What is different now is that Shakespeare is being made for the mass market, with one eye on the Oscars and another on the potentially vast video and CD-ROM market to follow. So the New Wave of Shakespeare films try to create a world that cinema audiences are already comfortable with, and that includes chase scenes, explosions, fights and gory deaths. . . .

The new films are not "Shakespeare, Men In Tights," as Russell Jackson of the Shakespeare Institute (and production consultant on all Branagh's Shakespeare films) puts it. Most are set in the 19th century—like Branagh's *Hamlet* and Trevor Nunn's *Twelfth Night*—"because the 19th century is a period which is romantically appealing but doesn't look like fancy dress."

The new Shakespeare films draw both upon the theatrical and cinematic traditions. Adrian Noble's *Midsummer Night's Dream* echoes Peter Brook's production in the 1960s—only a few minutes of which were filmed. "I think he is deliberately evoking[9] memories of the Peter Brook production," says Professor Wells, "but often to play around with it in a post-structural way." Branagh's *Hamlet* makes use of the long, uninterrupted takes in Olivier's (although he hates the comparisons that are so frequently drawn between them).

But while the New Shakespearians may look back over one shoulder to the greats of the past, their biggest task remains captivating the audiences of the present. Kenneth Branagh (as he explains below) . . . make[s] fewer concessions than most: his film [is] the full, no-line-cut-or-rewritten version [coming] in at a little under four hours; McKellen's *Richard III* is a brisk (one hour and 45 minutes), action-packed number, in which Shakespeare's lines are butchered as brutally as Richard knocks off his enemies.

Still, one wonders, on hearing Branagh grapple with lines like "I fingered their packet," whether McKellen's decision to chop unwieldy[10] lines and modernise outdated ones might not have been wiser. He is confident Shakespeare would have thought so, but Branagh argues that he'd rather use Shakespeare's actual words since they, for him, seem to say it all too superbly to paraphrase.

But in the movies, Branagh is the exception. Mainstream theatre has long been boldly experimental with Shakespeare, as have "fringe" films. Now, at last, major film makers have discovered that they can have fun with Shakespeare and that he's very forgiving.

"Many film critics hardly ever go to the theatre," says McKellen, "and they don't realise that every year there are several *Richard IIIs* on stage

---

7. **highbrow** intellectual
8. **avant-garde** unconventional; experimental
9. **evoking** bringing forth
10. **unwieldy** clumsy

which push the boundaries further. Now films are catching up, throwing caution to the wind and showing that you don't have to treat Shakespeare reverently to revere[11] him." . . .

## A brief history of Shakespeare in the movies

We will shortly be celebrating a century of Shakespeare on film. One of the first films ever made, in 1899, was Herbert Beerbohm Tree's *King John*— silent, of course—as was Sarah Bernhardt's *Hamlet* in 1900. If the concept of silent Shakespeare sounds silly, Professor Wells points out: "It shows that Shakespeare is not, as people sometimes erroneously[12] say, all in the words. Shakespeare was writing visuals as well as verbals, which is one reason that the plays translate so well, because their basic scenarios are strong ones—as the recent 'animated Shakespeare' showed."

But there hasn't been such a flurry of filming Shakespeare for the big screen with big names since the Forties and Fifties, when Olivier directed and starred in *Henry V, Hamlet* and *Richard III*, Orson Welles his *Macbeth*, and Marlon Brando played Mark Antony in Joseph Mankiewicz's *Julius Caesar*. Before that, in the Thirties, a youthful Olivier starred as Orlando in *As You Like It*, and an all-star cast including Mickey Rooney (as Puck) and James Cagney (as Bottom) did Max Reinhardt's sparkling *A Midsummer Night's Dream*.

Between that early Golden Age of Shakespeare films and the present renaissance, which is generally credited to have been set in motion by Branagh's *Henry V* in 1989 for, appropriately, Renaissance Films (following the footsteps of Olivier on two counts by starting with this play that Olivier made in 1944 to raise morale during the war and by directing it himself), there were a few scattered efforts such as Zeffirelli's *Taming of the Shrew* (1967) with Elizabeth Taylor and Richard Burton; *Romeo and Juliet* (1968) with unknowns Olivia Hussey and Leonard Whiting; Olivier's *Othello* in 1965; Tony Richardson's *Hamlet*, featuring the darling of the day Marianne Faithfull (1969); and Roman Polanski's *Macbeth* (1971, for Playboy Productions) . . . .

But the Sixties, Seventies and Eighties were a fertile time for Shakespeare on the small screen—particulary for lengthy history cycles, given names such as *An Age of Kings* (BBC 1960) and *The Wars of The Roses* (BBC 1964). The BBC also churned out a series of rather cheap-looking (though well played) adaptations throughout the Seventies and into the Eighties, but Trevor Nunn helmed[13] an impressive *Macbeth* for Thames in 1978, with Ian McKellen and Judi Dench.

---

11. **revere** love and respect
12. **erroneously** wrongly
13. **helmed** directed

But by the end of the Eighties Shakespeare was back in the cinemas, with Kenneth Branagh directing and starring in *Henry V*. Its success, particularly in the U. S., convinced the industry that the Bard was once again a worthwhile investment, and the following year Zeffirelli returned to familiar territory with his Mel Gibson-starring *Hamlet*. The presence of a big box-office name led to even more impressive grosses,[14] which no doubt accounts for the presence of American heartthrobs Denzel Washington and Keanu Reeves in Branagh's 1993 adaptation of *Much Ado About Nothing*. In the U. S. this fresh, breezy comedy made over $20m, an outstanding performance for an art-house picture.

[A 1995] Shakespearean adaptation reworked one of the great tragedies as an erotic thriller, presumably hoping to appeal to the Saturday night multiplex crowd. Meeting with tepid[15] reviews, Oliver Parker's *Othello*, despite all the sex, violence and drastic shortening, did not live up to expectations at the box office. But it was notable for featuring another compelling performance from the Bard-friendly Branagh, and also the screen's first genuinely black Othello, African-American actor Laurence Fishburne. Some critics carped[16] about the ruthless editing of the text and insertion of new scenes, but others maintained that such revisionism[17] is essential if Shakespeare is to survive.

---

14. **grosses**  monetary totals
15. **tepid**  lukewarm
16. **carped**  complained
17. **revisionism**  change; alteration

Lynne Heffley

# Allow Puck to Introduce Kids to Will

*Lynne Heffley's article examines a modern adaptation of*
A Midsummer Night's Dream *performed by the Los
Angeles Women's Shakespeare Company. The adaptation
is set in New York City and incorporates various elements
that give it a contemporary, urban edge.*

SHAKESPEARE'S blithe[1] forest frolic,[2] *A Midsummer Night's Dream*, is a
great way to introduce children to a classic theater work, and the respected
Los Angeles Women's Shakespeare Company's new adaptation is especially
family friendly, according to artistic director Lisa Wolpe.

"I think it's Shakespeare's most accessible[3] play," Wolpe said, "and in our
contemporary setting, it's even more accessible." . . . In this updated, urban
adaptation of a tale about meddling fairies and tangled romance, Fairy King
Oberon, Fairy Queen Titania, mischievous sprite Puck, a troupe of buffoonish
thespians[4] and comically bewitched lovers exist in a "modern, New York
dreamscape" under neon city lights.

"We've got some great diva singers in the cast" to sing gospel and
rhythm and blues, Wolpe said. "The clothing is contemporary and the
dance style is a kind of hip-hop. We haven't changed the language, except
in certain moments. For instance, instead of referring to Athens, it's
Manhattan. Instead of happening in the wood, it happens in the 'hood."
Wolpe, a former New York resident, said she took her inspiration from
memories of the city's vivid night life.

---

1. **blithe** cheerful
2. **frolic** merry play
3. **accessible** easily understood
4. **buffoonish thespians** clownish actors

"At 3 o'clock in the morning, it was very magical, with the neons lit and the streets alive with characters. I thought, let's have the fairies emerge out of the night and have the magic become a city magic, expressed through music and dance."

Wolpe and her 6-year-old company have won critical acclaim for productions of *Romeo and Juliet*, *Richard III*, *Measure for Measure* and other Shakespeare classics. *A Midsummer Night's Dream*, however, is her favorite, she said.

"The challenge is that it's done so often. But that also frees me to take some liberties with it. I didn't feel I had to do it with Arthur Rackham[5] fairies, real flowers on the stage, and all that. So, it's a bit of a concept piece, but it's still filled with the kinds of love and magic and laughter that are essential to the play."

The casting of the fairies is another innovation. Wolpe chose a double cast of more than 20 girls, ages 5 to 15, all members of the locally based Dance for Self-Esteem Ensemble, for the fairy roles.

According to the company's artistic director, Syni Patterson, it's a dream come true for the ethnically mixed young dancers, who auditioned for the roles.

"They're singing, dancing, acting—it's just an incredible opportunity they have to grow in grace and dignity, and all the things it means to be a young woman," said Patterson, whose mission is to instill[6] in students a passion for positive thinking along with a passion for dance.

Doing the play feeds heavily into that goal, Patterson noted. "The girls get to see up-close professional work—women directing, acting, building the set. And they have the chance to work with all these gifted and talented women, who are so generous and kind to them."

"It's a celebration of women and girls working together on stage," Wolpe said, "and it's a real accomplishment for our company."

---

5. **Arthur Rackham** (1867–1939) English artist known for his delicate and imaginative illustrations of fairies, gnomes, witches, and other such figures

6. **instill** put in gradually

Jennifer Lee
Carrell

# How the Bard Won the West

*Roping cattle and taming wild horses were not the only things cowboys did out West during the nineteenth century. They read Shakespeare. They not only read him, they quoted him and performed his plays alongside coal miners, trappers, ladies, and outlaws. Jennifer Lee Carrell, a Shakespeare scholar, explores the playwright's popularity in the wild West of the 1800s.*

Sometime late in 1863, a tall, thin man rode out of an Army camp in the Wyoming territory and headed across the prairie. He was just under 60 years old, one of the greatest scouts and Indian fighters, a man from whom Kit Carson took orders. It was the wild places that Jim Bridger liked best; following strange tales into the unknown, he was probably the first white man to see the Great Salt Lake. At that moment, however, he was headed toward people, not away from them. Not too far off, the Oregon Trail snaked westward across the landscape. Traffic had dwindled by 1863, but this "trail" still ranked as a highway by the standards of men such as Bridger; you could hardly follow its hard-packed earth so much as a day without running across somebody. That was exactly why Bridger was headed there.

He was looking to do some trading. What he had to offer was a yoke of cattle, then worth about $125, or almost a month of his wages as an Army scout. What Bridger wanted, and what he thought he could get from a wagon train, was a book. And not just any book, but the book that an Army officer had told him was the best ever written. He wanted Shakespeare.

Bridger's quest might sound unlikely, but all over the American West trappers, cowboys, miners, outlaws, proper ladies, . . . and Army officers regarded Shakespeare with a familiar ease and delight that might astonish the average American in the late 20th century. The history of the West, in fact, is a history of playing Shakespeare, of playing *with* Shakespeare, in what now may seem peculiar places and surprising ways.

Bridger, for instance, got what he wanted: someone, going west in wagons that could hold only the most necessary and precious possessions, had brought along a volume of Shakespeare. Out on the prairie, that someone judged the book not quite so precious as a yoke of cattle. For the additional sum of $40 per month, Bridger hired a German boy to read his new book to him. For though he could speak English, French, Spanish and a dozen Indian languages, and though he could draw, freehand, highly accurate maps of the West, Bridger could not read.

He could listen, however, and listen he did. Bridger was already well known as a storyteller. Because he sometimes embellished[1] the already extraordinary natural marvels of the West, and because writers and others made up wild tales and attributed them to him, he also had a growing though undeserved reputation as a liar. That winter, however, he added to his repertoire:[2] from then on he could quote Shakespeare at length. The prospect of an old mountain man spouting Shakespeare now seems more fantastic than the same man spinning tales about salt lakes, glass mountains and hot- and cold-running rivers. Nonetheless, Bridger came to know Shakespeare's cadences[3] of speech so well that his own speech could slide through the poet's rhythms, especially the insults. One of Bridger's tricks was to insert his own oaths into Shakespeare, so that his audience did not know where the playwright stopped and the mountain man began.

In search of the places that Bridger and others once took Shakespeare, I find myself heading off the main roads, and then off-road altogether. Up in Colorado's Gunnison County, I wind north through a wide valley filled with quaking aspen and tall trumpet flowers. Passing beneath the mountain whose sky-hungry spires gave the town of Gothic its name, the road bounces up over a pass and creeps into a darker forest of pine and spruce. This is country that in summer is still best covered on horseback.

But I am horseless, so when I give up on the car, I set off on foot. For somewhere up here, say century-old documents that briefly sound more like *The Hobbit* than legal records, "at the foot of the Treasure Mountain" there lies a mine called Shakespeare.

It was not a spectacularly rich mine, but it was respectable. Two years after it was located in 1879, the last of its original owners, John Blewett, sold out for $30,000. Blewett may have revered the Bard, but he didn't spend all his free time reading. Having sold his rights to the mine, he promptly made his way down to Gothic and won a shooting contest.

---

1. **embellished** exaggerated
2. **repertoire** collection
3. **cadences** rhythmical sounds

The name is scattered all over the West: "Shakespeare" names a town and a canyon in New Mexico, a mountaintop in Nevada, a reservoir in Texas and a glacier in Alaska. But it was the miners who most often staked Shakespeare to the earth. Nineteenth-century claims called Shakespeare dotted the landscape of Colorado and spilled over into Utah. The mines that still scar Western mountains now seem a curious honorific[4] for a great poet. Yet, Shakespeare takes his place among heroes and sweethearts.

In their quest for distinctive names, the miners delved into the Bard's stories. Colorado sports mines called Ophelia, Cordelia and Desdemona. There is even a "Timon of Athens," revealing that some prospectors dug into remote corners of Shakespeare as well as remote corners of North America, because *Timon* is one of Shakespeare's least-known plays. It is a fitting name for a mine, though, because the play's hero—a mad, bankrupt misanthrope[5]—accidentally discovers "yellow, glittering, precious gold" while digging in the forest for roots.

I did not, in the end, find the valley where modern survey maps and ancient mining records suggest the remains of Blewett's mine lie. Far to the south, however, I did find an entire town called Shakespeare. By 1879, Ralston, New Mexico, was short on respectability, having been the site of a diamond-mine hoax that had produced a bank failure, a suicide and substantial losses for investors. In April of that year, therefore, Col. William G. Boyle renamed the town Shakespeare. He already owned the Stratford Hotel, and Main Street was familiarly known as Avon Avenue; soon after, Boyle organized the Shakespeare Gold and Silver Mining and Milling Company. The townsmen joined the trend, organizing the Shakespeare Guards to defend the place against Apache raids.

Shakespeare was more than a name to miners, however. During the gold rush, playgoing had a prominent place among the drinking, gambling and carrying on that was the miners' usual relief from hard and dangerous work. From Colorado to California, theaters that played Shakespeare more than any other playwright perched just across the street, or sometimes right upstairs, from the saloons and gambling halls . . . . All over the West, towns built elaborate gilt-and-plush theaters grandiosely[6] called opera houses. A few of these jewel-box theaters still survive in former boomtowns such as Nevada City, California; Tombstone, Arizona; and Aspen, Central City, and Leadville, Colorado. When theaters weren't available people gathered in saloons, hotel hallways or even tents to watch actors play on stages made of packing boxes or boards laid across billiard tables and lit by kerosene

---

4. **honorific** way of giving praise
5. **misanthrope** hater of people
6. **grandiosely** impressively

lanterns; in Calaveras County, California, actors performed on the stump of a giant redwood.

The greatest actors from the Eastern Seaboard played to packed houses on these stages. Edwin Booth (elder brother of John Wilkes Booth) played his first Shakespearean leads on the magnificent and makeshift stages of California. That this caliber[7] of actor regularly appeared in such venues might have been for adventure's sake, but it was also partly because there was fame and wealth to be found among the miners. In the 1850s, top actors could earn up to $3,000 a week in San Francisco; the best theaters in the East were offering only a tenth as much. But it was up in the boisterous camps that the actors struck gold. In places with names like Rattlesnake, Rough and Ready, Git-up-and-Git and Hangtown, theater tickets were bought with gold dust, and cheering miners tossed nuggets and bags of gold dust onto the stage at curtain call.

The first people to carry Shakespeare into the West were trappers, who threaded their way into the Rockies along the rivers on their quest for beaver. Mountain men were legendary for gathering around campfires to tell bear stories both hair-raising and hilarious. According to the recollections of trappers Joe Meek and Bill Hamilton, however, though they might indeed be swapping bear stories, they might just as well be sharing a little Shakespeare. Or they might even be doing both: after all, the Bard's most infamous stage direction, from *The Winter's Tale*, is "Exit pursued by a bear."

On the frontier, Shakespeare was not "Art" to be adored in silent, solitary reading; Shakespeare was a set of stories to be told aloud, language to be tasted, toyed with, tossed about over a campfire. Bridger is a case in point: after he bought his precious book, it never seems to have occurred to him to learn to read. What he wanted from the book was specifically what was in it. Like Bridger, other Westerners might get their Shakespeare out of books, but in books they did not let him stay. The 19th century was an age of oral storytelling and public speaking; if Shakespeare was taught at all, it was taught as oratory and recitation—then parts of the most basic schooling. Since Shakespeare was seen and heard more than read, no one needed much, if any, formal education to have at least a passing acquaintance with the works. Montana rancher Philip Ashton Rollins said that many ranch owners brought Shakespeare west with them. It was not unusual to see "a bunch of cowboys sitting on their spurs listening with absolute silence and concentration while somebody read aloud." Further, Shakespeare was popular because of the poetry, not in spite of it. After listening to the blood and thunder "dogs of war" speech in *Julius Caesar*, one top hand told Rollins, "Gosh! That fellow

---

7. **caliber** quality

Shakespeare could sure spill the real stuff. He's the only poet I ever seen what was fed on raw meat."

Among Westerners, the most popular Shakespearean plays were the tragedies and epic histories, with *Richard III, Hamlet, Othello, Macbeth* and *Romeo and Juliet* heading the list. Westerners, however, were not silenced into tongue-tied awe by high tragedy. Like Bridger—who was once heard to say that Falstaff (or "Mr. Full-stuff") liked beer a little too much for his own good and might have been better off with bourbon—cowboys, outlaws, miners and trappers embraced Shakespeare. They brought it to life, retelling it in a mix of remembered poetry and the teller's own salty language.

Along with the enthusiasm came irreverence. It was common in 19th-century American theater to follow the main play, no matter how profound, with a comic song, a dance, and finally a farce[8] in which the principal actors often reappeared. In Denver in 1859, a troupe followed *Richard III* with a polka and a farce called *Luck in a Name;* in San Francisco, *King Lear* was once followed by a dancing horse named Adonis. Sometimes the kind of mischief that led Bridger to alter Shakespeare's oaths took over the stage completely. Audiences loved farces with titles like *Hamlet and Egglet* and *Julius Sneezer,* and burlesque[9] Shakespeare was popular minstrel fare.

Westerners also delighted in creative casting. In Army camps, all-male performances were not uncommon. In Texas on the eve of the Mexican War, Lieut. Ulysses S. Grant was drafted into the role of Desdemona because he supposedly looked the part. Before opening night, however, his superiors had to send off to New Orleans for a real woman, because Grant failed to show "the proper sentiment." Great actresses playing Shakespearean heroes in serious productions were ticket-selling curiosities. The women's success led to the brief vogue[10] of having little girls play the major tragic roles; thus did Anna Maria Quinn, age 6, play Hamlet to a mostly adult male audience at San Francisco's Metropolitan Theater in 1854. In Deer Lodge, Montana, on the other hand, miners and cowboys were treated to the spectacle of an actress playing Juliet with an imitation Romeo: a "blockhead in every respect" reported one witness delighted by the wooden dummy outfitted with wig and red cambric gown, and even more by the parodic[11] performance that followed.

Because Shakespeare—as story or poetry or theater—was shared by so many people, it became a kind of imaginative meeting place. The readings organized by Bridger, for example, brought together an illiterate mountain man, a German boy and the well-educated Army officer who had first

---

8. **farce** broad comedy
9. **burlesque** comic
10. **vogue** fashion
11. **parodic** comically imitative

recommended the Bard. In the theater, there was no assumption that Shakespeare should be delivered in the plummy tones of the British upper class; audiences flocked to hear their favorite actors play Shakespeare in English heavily laden with German, Polish, French and Italian accents in addition to regional British, American and Australian inflections.

For all the intensity of their love affair with Shakespeare, Westerners had no monopoly on it. In 1849, what is still one of the bloodiest riots in American history broke out in New York City—over styles of acting Shakespeare. A vigorous style was said to be democratic and American, while more cerebral acting was said to be aristocratic and English. Enraged by a supposedly elitist[12] performance of *Macbeth*, a crowd of 10,000 surged outside the Astor Place Opera House (*Smithsonian*, October 1985). When the mob turned from hurling insults to hurling paving stones, the New York militia opened fire, shooting directly into the crowd; at least 22 people died and 150 others were wounded.

As the frontier straggled westward, the differences that had chafed[13] in crowded New York were stretched out across the continent; Westerners favored flamboyant acting while disdaining[14] polished elegance as snobbish and Eastern. Less than a year after the Astor Place Riot, Shakespeare arrived along with the forty-niners in the California goldfields, and by 1856, the Californians, too, were brawling over Shakespeare. In the West, though, it was not politics but the combination of characters acting badly and actors acting badly that provoked riots.

At a Sacramento performance of *Richard III*, the audience began to get restive[15] in the face of Richard's mounting evil and the actor's obvious incompetence. When at last Richard stabbed one of his victims in the back, the audience began tossing any and all handy garbage onto the stage: bags of flour and soot, old vegetables, a dead goose. At the request of the stage manager, the audience allowed Richard to reappear, but when he placed his sword in the hands of Lady Anne during the wooing scene, "one half the house, at least, asked that [the sword] might be plunged in his body," the Sacramento *Union* reported. The actor was finally driven from the stage by a "well directed pumpkin . . . with still truer aim, a potato relieved him of his cap, which was left upon the field of glory, among the cabbages."

In their noisy displays of pleasure and displeasure, Western audiences preserved and even heightened an exuberant tradition of theatergoing dating back to the Elizabethan audiences that Shakespeare knew. They

---

12. **elitist** superior; high-class
13. **chafed** rubbed the wrong way
14. **disdaining** looking down upon
15. **restive** restless

expected to enter into the spirit of play, and the same enthusiasm that could produce showers of either rotten vegetables or gold dust also provoked, at less frenzied moments, stamping, cheering, whistling and hooting, as well as quips and running commentary on the play, the players and the production.

This freewheeling audience participation had once been common all over America, but in the late 19th century Shakespearean theater was fast becoming an elite and stately affair in the East and in Europe. Western audiences preserved longer their right to play during the play. Appearing as Othello in 1886, Tommaso Salvini was so disturbed by the laughter and popping of champagne corks coming from "Silver King" Horace Tabor's personal box in Denver's Tabor Grand Opera House that he sent a note up during intermission threatening to stop the play if things in Box A did not quiet down. "My theater is a playhouse as much for the audience as for the actors," Tabor reportedly bellowed back. "If that Eyetalian wants to pray," Tabor fumed, "let him go to church."

Nonetheless, changing attitudes eventually traveled westward; Lawrence Levine of George Mason University, in Fairfax, Virginia, has speculated that Shakespeare's fall from popularity in America was caused by large-scale shifts in ideas about what is entertainment and what is art. When Shakespeare stopped being story and began to be art, it began to seem distant; when accuracy became more important than entertainment, it became boring; and when the language of Shakespeare ceased to be commonly heard aloud, it began to seem difficult. Beyond doubt, however, changing attitudes toward Shakespeare have resulted in what now looks like a paradox:[16] Shakespeare's popularity in the American West dwindled as the West was settled and ceased to be wild.

Shakespeare has not, however, disappeared from the West without a trace: it still shapes the myth of what we think the West was, or ought to have been. The novel that established the genre of the western, Owen Wister's *The Virginian* (published in 1902), features an aloof hero who is a dead shot and a deeply honorable man. He is also prone[17] to quoting Shakespeare; the poet's lyricism captivates him. "The singing masons building roofs of gold," he says at one point, quoting from *King Henry V*. "Ain't that a fine description of bees a-workin'? . . . Puts 'em right before yu', and is poetry without bein' foolish." Following the novelists, Hollywood, too, has borrowed from Shakespeare in shaping our idea of the West that was. The film *Broken Lance* (1954), for instance, tells *King Lear* in the guise of a western, while *Jubal* (1956) reshapes *Othello*.

---

16. **paradox** contradiction
17. **prone** inclined

Today up in Leadville, you can, as I did, climb onto the stage of the Tabor Opera House and stand in front of the painted scenery that once backed *Romeo and Juliet.* Facing the plush seats that curve toward you, you can let your voice roll out into the hushed and waiting darkness on the cadences of Shakespeare. In the ghost town of Shakespeare, you can, as I did, duck out of the New Mexico sun into the shade of the Stratford Hotel's long narrow dining room, where the desert wind will send the fine silt of crumbling adobe drifting over your skin and through your hair; there you can listen to the stories that the town's present owners, Janaloo Hill and Manny Hough, have spent a lifetime collecting from old-timers.

Yet Shakespeare is more than a ghost in the West. After the Bard ceased to be part of their everyday life, Westerners began to pioneer the Shakespeare festival. Every summer tourists descend upon the towns of Ashland, Oregon, and Cedar City, Utah, to gorge themselves on Shakespeare brilliantly brought to life in faux[18] Elizabethan theaters set down among the forests of the Pacific Northwest and the red rock canyons of the Southwest. Scattered over the West as well are productions aimed more at local audiences, such as the Colorado Shakespeare Festival in Boulder and the Grand Canyon Shakespeare Festival in Flagstaff, Arizona. In Boulder, you can spend a summer's evening picnicking on a wide lawn and then wander into a Greek-style amphitheater hewn out of local red stone. As the sky deepens to sapphire edged by the strange, stark shapes of the Flatiron Mountains that loom behind the set, you can be swept away to some far country on the tide of Shakespeare, sharing the laughter of a thousand Coloradans as Beatrice baits Benedick, or shivering with the hiss of indrawn breath as Romeo forever drinks poison a scant moment too early to see that Juliet still breathes. But here, as I listen to the crowds dispersing downhill through the trees, the laughter and the sorrow are tinged with surprise: that Shakespeare is here, that it is so good, that they have enjoyed it so much. In the frontier West, the fact that Shakespeare tells good stories, and that those stories should be told well in the West, was no surprise at all—at least not to Westerners. From Jim Bridger, to the forty-niners, to the cowboys, the old wanderers would hardly recognize anything in the modern cities that rise on the plains and mountains, strung out like glittering beads along the Interstate freeways. Yet they might recognize and be glad of one thing on such a summer night: Shakespeare still plays well under Western skies.

---

18. **faux** fake